INWARD BOUND

ALSO BY SAM KEEN
Fire in the Belly
Your Mythic Journey
(WITH ANNE VALLEY-FOX)
To a Dancing God
Faces of the Enemy

INWARD BOUND

EXPLORING THE GEOGRAPHY
OF YOUR EMOTIONS

Sam Keen

BANTAM BOOKS
New York Toronto London Sydney Auckland

INWARD BOUND

A Bantam Book / published by arrangement with the author

PRINTING HISTORY

Originally published as *What To Do When You're Bored and Blue*
Widen Books edition published 1980
Bantam edition / June 1992

Grateful acknowledgment is made for permission to reprint the following: The Social Readjustment Rating Scale is reprinted with permission from *Journal of Psychosomatic Research*, 11, Holmes, T. H., and Rahe, R. H. Copyright © 1967, Pergamon Press plc.; Excerpt from *The Myth of Freedom* by Chogyam Trungpa. Copyright © 1976 by Chogyam Trungpa. Reprinted by arrangement with Shambhala Publications, Inc., 300 Massachusetts Avenue, Boston, MA 02115.

Book design by Terry Karydes.

Library of Congress Cataloging-in-Publication Data

Keen, Sam.
   Inward bound : exploring the geography of your emotions / Sam Keen.
      p.   cm.
   Rev. ed. of: What to do when you're bored and blue. 1980.
   Includes bibliographical references and index.
   ISBN 0-553-35388-8
   1. Boredom.   2. Depression, Mental.   I. Keen, Sam. What to do when
you're bored and blue.   II. Title.
BF575.B67K43   1992
158'.1—dc20   91-45215
                                                                   CIP

Published simultaneously in the United States and Canada

Bantam Books are published by Bantam Books, a division of Bantam
Doubleday Dell Publishing Group, Inc. Its trademark, consisting of the
words "Bantam Books" and the portrayal of a rooster, is Registered in U.S.
Patent and Trademark Office and in other countries. Marca Registrada.
Bantam Books, 666 Fifth Avenue, New York, New York 10103.

PRINTED IN THE UNITED STATES OF AMERICA
FFG   0 9 8 7 6 5 4 3 2 1

CONTENTS

INTRODUCTION

NO RAINBOW WITHOUT BLUES

As early as I can remember I wanted my life to be a rainbow of vivid experiences. All technicolor. No gray, brown, or shades of night. I wanted to taste, touch, and try everything, to stuff myself with the kaleidoscope of human possibilities. Better to burn than rust. Even my name—Keen—suggested that my DNA and my destiny was to be on the cutting edge. I wanted to be a perpetual explorer, always pushing the limits. My mind was sharp and restless, and I honed my doubts into questions that I flung at anyone who seemed prematurely satisfied. Twenty-five years before jogging was invented I began running, determined to create a lean body that was at home in motion. I felt the need to be near the edge of danger. I wrestled, climbed mountains, skin-dived, rode motorcycles. After ascending the academic ladder (Ph.D. and full professorship with tenure), I abandoned the security I had earned and became a free-lance lecturer and writer. I moved to California so I could immerse myself in the happenings of the late 1960s—revolution for the hell of it, encounter groups, psychedelic consciousness, sensory awareness, etc. I was determined that midlife was not going to catch me turning drab and bovine. At the time, I told my wife that if I ever said "I am content" she would know I had squelched the flame that was my spirit. Give me intensity or give me death.

Needless to say, I was not a comfortable person. In moments of candor friends would hint that it was exciting but exhausting to be in my ambience. Too much air and fire, not enough earth and water. My astrologically oriented friends nodded their heads knowingly and said: "Just what we would expect from a double Sagittarius with his moon in . . ." I attributed it all to Scottish genes, driving curiosity, and a lust for life.

I was totally unprepared when I crashed, burned, and plunged into darkness. A divorce after seventeen years of marriage and a few frantic years of trying to be a carefree bachelor landed me in the middle of what medieval mystics described as "the dark night of the soul" and modern psychologists (with less poetry and less soul) prefer to call "depression" or "midlife crisis." Since I have written about the process of confronting my personal demons and beginning again in *The Passionate Life* and in *Fire in the Belly*, I will not repeat the story here. Suffice it to say that the obscure ache of depression began to disappear when I ceased running from my pain and became interested in discriminating between the nuances of the "negative" emotions that make up the geography of the night country of the psyche. I began to study the differences between fatigue, boredom, depression, grief, despair, etc.

As I became more expert in being an objective witness to the changing topography of my emotions, I began to observe how I would do anything to maintain a high level of dramatic intensity in my life. I was so addicted to intensity that it didn't seem to matter whether I was in the pits or the heights so long as something extreme was happening. Facing challenges, pushing my mind and body to the point of exhaustion by excessive work or play, seemed better than settling into middle-class tranquillity.

One day I found myself sitting in my living room, looking at the waves in the ocean, and being gently bored. I couldn't think of anything that really excited me or anything I wanted to do. I wasn't deeply depressed, simply captured by inertia. My immediate and natural impulse was to force myself into action. Do something—eat, go to the movies, call up a friend, start a new project, pick a fight with my wife. Anything to escape the void. Instead I did something highly unusual for me—I did nothing other than sit quietly and study the contours of my boredom.

Lo and behold, I discovered that the monster of boredom I had spent a lifetime running to avoid was more interesting than terrible. Benign, even friendly, a respite from my frantic busyness. As I allowed my metabolism to slow down I learned to savor the sensations of ebb tide. Lying fallow I re-collected my life, did a kind of inventory of the satisfactions and dissatisfactions, and began to ask myself what I wanted in the future. It wasn't long before I became a connoisseur of that range of "blue" feelings I had previously lumped together under the name of "boredom." As I slowed down, my imagination began to blossom and new desires sprung from exhausted ground. A wealth of feelings sprouted where before there was only willpower and overdrive.

Gradually, I began to experience the promise that is a common theme in myth and folklore—we discover beauty only when we embrace the beast. Where we stumble and fall, there we find the gold. Beneath the fault lies the virtue. The stone the builders reject becomes the cornerstone. The treasure is hidden in the trash. Authentic happiness is only possible when we allow ourselves to experience the full range of human emotions, including boredom, fear, grief, anger, and despair.

Increasingly, people within what we self-servingly call "the developed" nations of the world have become addicted to highly consumptive styles of life that are dependent on constantly stimulated nervous systems and economies. We are busy, busy, busy. As the most "successful" men and women in our society are now working fifty- and sixty-hour weeks, it is ironic to remember that as recently as the 1960s sociologists were predicting a leisure revolution. The problem of the 1990s was supposed to be that we would have difficulty adjusting to the twenty-hour workweek. Instead we have become a nation of speed freaks, Type A personalities, hooked on the idea that there is something intrinsically valuable in change and "progress." The moment we experience a downturn, we fear depression and try to find ways to stimulate "growth." We seem to have completely lost the wisdom that led the leaders of biblical times to decree that we should rest and celebrate one day each week and allow the land to lie fallow every seventh year. (I note in passing that Word Finder on my computer does not contain "fallow.")

My encounter with boredom and exploration of the spectrum of blue emotions convinced me that emotional and spiritual wholeness requires a psychological sabbath—a time and place of disengagement. Today's paper brings word that Dr. Franz Halberg of the University of Minnesota's Chronobiological Laboratories is convinced by empirical evidence that human beings are genetically programmed for seven-day rhythmic cycles. (*The New York Times*, 9/8/91, p. 15.) It has taken me a long time to discover the obvious: constant activity and the quest for excitement may exhaust the energies necessary for enjoyment of a full life.

There are several reasons I have chosen boredom as the Ariadne's thread that can best guide us on an inward-bound expedition to the center of the psyche. Any repressed emotion festers, grows septic, and contributes to a dis-ease that can only be healed by allowing the forbidden feeling into awareness. We can't recover an emotion whose existence we have denied. Furthermore, the realm of emotion (like a nation) "cannot long exist half-slave and half-free." When we keep a whole class of emotions in bondage, all other emotions will suffer. Boredom is taboo in our extroverted and activity-addicted culture. When I went to the library to study the literature of boredom, I found there was none. Depression and identity crises are popular maladies, but boredom is scarcely mentioned by modern psychologists. Could it be that nobody has suffered boredom since Pascal called ennui the major problem of mankind? For a while I wondered if I had been suffering from a disease like leprosy that belonged to a former age. Then I realized I had stumbled on a neglected and unexplored emotion that was the key to recovery of emotional fullness. When I first discovered that the "in" emotions in our time—anger and grief, guilt and shame—had all been well explored, I felt a little like the debutante who came out late in the season and couldn't find a cause to support because "all the good diseases had been taken." Lucky for me, nobody wanted boredom. Being a frequenter of thrift shops and swap meets, I knew an overlooked treasure when I saw one. I choose the path that begins with boredom because it is *the* undiagnosed dis-ease from which "normal" people suffer and the cure is readily available.

Fortunately for humankind, the road to hell is narrow and the highway to heaven is broad. There is a single path to sickness and a thousand ways to health. All you have to do to get worse is to keep narrowing your horizons, your arteries, your mind, your enthusiasms, your community, your compassion. And to get better all you have to do is open up to the multitudinous wonders and healing balms within, without, and around. Start unwinding the tangled string of your dis-ease and knots (the nots) in your spirit will loosen.

Many people never get started on the inward-bound journey because they wake up one day realizing they are emotionally poor and demand to be made emotionally rich immediately. When we discover our dis-ease we naturally want instant cures.

But the psyche doesn't work like that. When we have been long addicted to alcohol, drugs, work, bad relationships, etc., we cannot immediately transcend our emotionally stunted lives. There are no authentic rags-to-riches stories in the realm of the spirit. It takes time to explore and recover the full range of feelings we have spent years denying and ignoring. In developing emotional literacy, we must begin with abc before we can reach xyz.

Begin where you are rather than where you would like to be. Real spiritual journeys begin in the mud, the desert, the swamp, the wasteland, not in the seventh heaven. To recover fullness of feeling, begin with the emptiness of feeling. Begin by exploring numbness, boredom, confusion, ambivalence, and depression—the gray, dappled, and blue emotions. They will lead you through red-hot anger and searing grief to the center of life, where you will find bursting golden buds, upspringing green, and royal purple. The best way to a technicolor life is the willingness to experience the full spectrum. In the beginning of the journey you need only trust that there are no rainbows without blues.

PART

1

BOREDOM, BLAHS, AND BLUES: THE GEOGRAPHY OF NIGHT COUNTRY

CHAPTER 1

THE BOREDOM EPIDEMIC

Boredom is our number one social disease. It's growing in epidemic proportions. The closer we get to the prepackaged world of the mall, the more we are engulfed by psychic smog.

Unfortunately, boredom is not dramatic like cancer. It appears to be a minor-league demon, gray and anonymous. There is no Anti-Boredom Week, no Crusade Against Tedium, no Boredom Anonymous, no Foundation for the Elimination of Monotony. But the amorphous blob creeps over our land like a giant fungus in a grade-B science fiction movie. It devours our innocent enthusiasms and destroys our dreams. It insinuates itself into any ho-hum corner of our lives that has been prepared by fatigue. And the plague is mostly invisible because it paralyzes our powers of

---

WE SUFFER MORE FROM A VACUUM THAN A THORN IN THE FLESH.

perception even as it invades our psyches. So many of us suffer from it that we consider it normal, part of the inevitable atmosphere of modern life.

The fish doesn't know it is swimming in water. We have learned to accept tedious jobs, depressing cities, deadly bureaucracies, the television wasteland, and hopeless politics as just the way things are. Lively people, full of sap and sass, content with simplicity and few things, are rare as Shaker furniture. Wisdom has become an antique virtue, to be studied in the tintypes of great men and women of former ages. And wonder, which ancient philosophers celebrated as the aim and reward of a good human life, never makes the cover of *Rolling Stone* or *Newsweek*.

The blahs have us. The Sisyphus strain. The disease from inner space. Some vampire is quietly sucking away the lifeblood of our enthusiasm (from the Greek *entheos*, "inspired by a god") and hope—that spirit that former ages called "the soul." Most frightening, we allow our vitality to ebb away with scarcely a protest. Boredom may become such a natural part of modern technological society that we don't notice our dis-ease, or accept it passively. And die "not with a bang but a whimper."

How is it with you?

Perhaps you wake up one morning, and for no particular reason it is February in your soul. Blue Monday. The tide is out. Nothing is visible except mud flats. There isn't much pain, just a great and aching emptiness. And restlessness. The excitement has ebbed away from your life. Only a littered line of memories is left along the shore to mark the receding tide of your passion. You think

WHAT IS THE MOST IMPORTANT THING THAT HASN'T HAPPENED?

about your job, your marriage, the vacation you are going to take in August—everything seems stale and tasteless. Nothing matters much. You have no burning dreams or lively hopes. Not even outrage. You go through the day automatically, by the numbers, without feeling. Same old rat race.

When did you lose it? It is hard to remember.

Or maybe the boredom began the week after you retired or the children left for college and, suddenly, nobody needed you anymore. You tried to fill your days with hobbies, but time hung heavy. You did make-work around the house, joined a club, played golf three days a week. But when you weren't busy, that nameless sadness came over you and the future seemed to stretch before you like a sterile desert.

Or maybe you work at Electric Hose and Rubber Company, the three-to-eleven shift. You've been there seven years and have some seniority, but you are still young. Lately the monotony has been getting you down. After cutting and bundling 12,000 Chevrolet heater hoses, or watching an extruder squeeze out an endless ribbon of polyvinyl chloride pipe, your spirit feels deadened. Maybe it's just job fatigue. But then why do you feel so depressed, so much at a dead end?

Or maybe you are in teenage limbo. At school it's the same old thing every day. Like a prison. Eight 45-minute periods—including lunch and study hall. A curriculum and teachers tell you what you must learn for your own good. And after school, there is not much to do. So you hang out and smoke a joint or two.

Or maybe you are unemployed. You know it's not your fault, but you can't help feeling low about yourself. The day stretches ahead. What will you do? Read the paper. Maybe something good will turn up in the classifieds. Then wait till noon for the

TO BE AVERAGE YOU MUST CUT YOUR LONGING SHORT.

phone call from the contractor who just might have a job. In the afternoon you walk downtown and try to look busy. You resist the impulse to have a drink or look at TV until after dark. You are not going to sink to that.

If you are like most Americans you will ignore your boredom and hope it will go away. Or take up a hobby. Or have an affair. Or get divorced. Or start a new business. Or keep busy. Or eat to fill up the void. When none of these works you will fall into depression and wonder what's the matter with you. (Think of boredom as the common cold of the psyche and depression as pneumonia.) If you can afford it and aren't afraid of introspection you will seek psychiatric help. If you can't, you will get your physician to prescribe tranquilizers or mood elevators. Or you will drink. Or try to tough it out.

And you will feel alone. But you are not. Accurate statistics are hard to come by, but we can estimate from the dramatic increase in suicide attempts and sales of antidepressant drugs that boredom and depression will likely strike half of the population at some time in their lives. Psychiatrists report that most patients nowadays arrive in their consulting rooms not with raw pain but with a severe case of emptiness. "Doctor, I just don't feel anything. Something is missing and I don't know what it is. There must be more to life than this."

Modern literature warned us of the spiritual malaise long before psychiatric clinics were inundated with depressed patients. In 1936, Georges Bernanos in *Diary of a Country Priest* warned:

WHAT DO YOU WANT, MORE OR LESS?

The world is eaten up by boredom (ennui). To perceive this needs a little preliminary thought: you can't see it all at once. It is like dust. You go about and never notice it, you breathe it in, you eat and drink it. It is sifted so fine, it doesn't even grit on your teeth. But stand still for an instant and there it is, coating your face and hands. To shake off this drizzle of ashes you must be forever on the go. . . . I wonder if man has ever before experienced this contagion, this leprosy of boredom, an aborted despair, a shameful form of despair in some way like the fermentation of a Christianity in decay. . . . If ever our species is to perish it will die of boredom, of stale disgust. (As for instance the world wars of today, which would seem to show such prodigious human activity, are in fact indictments of a growing apathy of humanity. In the end, at certain stated periods, they will lead huge flocks of resigned sheep to be slaughtered.)

T. S. Eliot sketched the outline of the modern wasteland and showed us in J. Alfred Prufrock a man whose enthusiasm had fled:

I have seen them all already
The mornings, evenings, afternoons.
I have measured out my life in coffee spoons.

Hemingway provided the litany for a world where the experiences of the void replaced both hope and satisfaction. In "A Clean, Well-Lighted Place" he tells the story of an old man who

---

WHEN YOU'RE FED UP, IS SOMETHING EATING YOU?

has failed at everything, even suicide. He sits in a well-lit café for a moment before going out again into the night, and his life is summed up in a refrain that is a parody of the ancient prayer: "Our *nada* [Spanish for "nothing"] who art in *nada, nada* be thy name. . . ."

Samuel Beckett showed us the absurdity in *Waiting for Godot*. One bum asks the other: "Do you believe in the life to come?" "Mine always was," he replies. Paddy Chayevsky gave us an unforgettable vignette in *Marty* where two young men, hanging out on a Saturday night with nothing to do, keep asking each other:

> *What do you want to do, Marty?*
> *I don't know. What do you want to do, Angie?*
> *I don't know, Marty. What do you want to do?*

Boredom is doubly difficult to diagnose and cure because it is a closet disease. We are ashamed of it. Like guilt or shame we hide it behind a curtain of silence and denial. I found in conducting interviews for this book that most people protest too much: "I'm *never* bored." I asked one beautiful young mother if she was ever bored. "Never," she replied, "I'm always doing something. I don't have time." A week later she called me and asked if we could talk again. "When you first asked me if I was ever bored I denied it," she said. "But when I thought about it I realized I was bored all the time but I felt too embarrassed to admit it. I feel guilty. What right do I have to feel bored? I have everything, a beautiful house, a child. I travel to exotic places. I could take a job if I wanted, or even have an affair. I don't have any excuse for being bored. I have

---

EXTROVERTS TURN OUT FOR THINGS. INTROVERTS TURN IN TOWARD DREAMS.

no restrictions. But I don't really enjoy my life. I'm ashamed of myself. Here is all the beauty and preciousness of life and I'm not appreciating it! I feel lifeless. I just don't have enthusiasm for anything."

Americans are particularly phobic about boredom. We see ourselves as go-getters and the right to the pursuit of happiness is guaranteed us by law. By industry and imagination we have created a society richer in things than any past society. Most of us live in material luxury that medieval kings would have envied. In fact, we have democratized the dis-ease of kings. Everyone now can afford ennui.

To get a true picture of how much our lives are shaped by boredom, we have to look at its secondary effects—all the ways we spend our substance in trying to escape from this monster we deny is chasing us. The frenzy of our flight (and the strategies we use to avoid the void) gives us a true index of how much we fear what the early Christian monks referred to as "the demon of noontide." What price do we pay to maintain our false self-image as robust, never-bored-a-day-in-our-lives, on-top-of-it-all extroverts? What is the hidden cost of denying our boredom? Here are some of our substitutes, our favorite ways of dodging boredom:

Keeping busy. (The devil finds work for idle hands.) Stay on the go. Keep moving. Work and produce. We are what we do. If you are retired or find yourself with leisure, get a "hobby."

Speed. Americans are caught in perpetual motion. Our favorite drugs are caffeine and sugar. Never let the body, the psyche, or

---

THE LAW OF ECONOMIC AND PSYCHOLOGIC GRAVITY: WHAT GOES UP MUST COME DOWN. OR MANIA INVITES DEPRESSION.

the economy slow down. Stimulate. We are addicted to our own adrenaline. Speed freaks.

Consume. Eat. Fill the void. If any desire arises, satiate it with instant food, sex, or the latest gadget. Go to the mall.

Keep entertained. Fill up your time. Plug your nervous system into a radio or TV.

And what are the *results* of our flight from boredom? What price our denial of our dis-ease?

Fatigue. We are always tired. Our nervous systems and economy are exhausted by a diet of artificial stimulants. Speed freaks wear out young. We are suffering from a massive energy crisis. At the psychological level it is called depression. At the economic-political level it is called recession, stagnation, readjustment. But a depression by any other name smells just the same. And our addiction to stimulation as a way of life blinds us to our drugs and blinds us to the possible joys of a slower "steady-state" way of life. All our anxieties are focused on maintaining our "energy" sources. The manic-depressive cycle *is* the American way of life. Psychic, spiritual, economic exhaustion is the flip side of the drive for unbroken intensity, progress, "growth." The rule we follow is Satchel Paige's: "Don't never look back, 'cause something might be gaining on you."

Violence. Our love affair with violence springs from our desperate need to make our exhausted systems feel something. We would rather smash things and people than face our emptiness.

Violence comes in many forms:

CRIME IS A MOOD-ALTERING DRUG.

1. Divorce. We tear the fabric of the family. Nearly half of us have cut and run rather than continue to till the soil of fallow marriages. We have no faith that we must wait through the sterile winter before new life will appear. We demand that our relationships always be "interesting," "exciting," "growing."

2. Drugs stimulate the deadened psyche and imagination. Grass to make green the fields of imagination burned out by "education" and work. Amphetamines and "uppers" elevate the moods of those who cannot stand the depths. Alcohol deadens the pain of the loss of passion and puts our conscience to troubled sleep.

3. Juvenile delinquents horrify us because they practice what the media preach—violence pays. Why should we be surprised that after watching 25,000 murders and an equal number of miscellaneous crimes on TV our young people get hooked on violence? Here is what the playwright Arthur Miller says about it in an article, "The Bored and the Violent."[1]

No one knows what "causes" delinquency. Having spent some months in the streets with boys of an American gang, I came away with . . . a single, overwhelming conviction—that the problem underneath is boredom. . . . People no longer seem to know why they are alive; existence is simply a string of near-experiences marked off by periods of stupefying spiritual and psychological stasis, and the good life is basically an amused one. . . . The delinquent is stuck with his boredom, stuck inside, stuck to it, until for two or three minutes he "lives"; he goes on a raid around the corner and feels the thrill of risking his skin or

WAR IS AN EXPENSIVE CHEAP THRILL.

his life as he smashes a bottle filled with gasoline on some other kid's head. In a sense, it is his trip to Miami. It makes his day. It is his shopping tour. It gives him something to talk about for a week. It is life. Standing around with nothing coming up is as close to dying as you can get. Unless one grasps the power of boredom, the threat of it to one's existence, it is impossible to "place" the delinquent as a member of the human race.

And delinquency is only Little Leaque violence, not even big enough for the NFL. In big league violence the play-off is between suicide and war.

4. Suicide is violence for the introvert; war is violence for the extrovert. The suicide rate among teenagers, the unemployed, and the retired is soaring. We murder the self because of disgust at our unlived lives. When our capacity for hope has been exhausted, some of us prefer to die all at once rather than by inches. Without work or worth, life is empty. Better to take the "only way out" than face the void. Certain phrases keep popping up in suicide notes: "I'm tired." "I can't go on." "I've lost my nerve." "There is nothing left to live for." "This is the only thing left that I can do." "I just want to rest." "My soul is dead." "I have felt myself slipping."

5. War is the final distraction. Nations regularly sacrifice their blood for "adventure" disguised as honor. Violence makes us feel alive. War gives us an occasion for heroism and intensity. When we get too secure, boredom creeps in; we want the excitement that war gives us. (The rate of individual suicides drops in

---

HAPPINESS IS BEING CONSUMED; FIRE OR PASSION, NOT EATING OR OWNING.

wartime.) Warfare is relief from tedium. Reflecting on the exaltation of the Vienna crowds in August 1914, Trotsky wrote, "The people whose lives day in and day out pass in a monotony of hopelessness are many: they are the mainstay of modern society. The alarm of mobilizations breaks into their lives like a promise; the familiar and long-hated is overthrown, and the new and unusual reigns in its place. Changes still more incredible are in store for them in the future. For better or worse? For better of course—what can seem worse . . . than normal conditions."[2]

6. Illness. How much sickness is an escape? Every hypochondriac knows it is better to suffer than face the void. One of Faulkner's characters says: "Between nothingness and grief, I will choose grief." Illness is a break in the routine.

Some specialists in psychosomatic medicine suggest that cancer and other life-threatening diseases may sometimes be ways for novelty to be introduced into stuck lives. The disease provokes a crisis: change or die!

Certainly we all recognize how much we do daily violence to ourselves. We worry, fill ourselves with constant anxiety. It is the unusual person who can tolerate happiness for more than three days at a time.

Why do we have this love affair with suffering? What is worse than pain? Nothingness perhaps. We court stress and dis-ease rather than risk contentment. Why are we so threatened by psychological, spiritual, physical health?

When we begin to tally the cost of our "normal" efforts to escape a vacuum of meaning in our lives, it is clear that it is time

---

No speed demon can outrun the devil.

to bring our dis-ease out of the closet. Bertrand Russell said, "Boredom is a vital problem for the moralist, since at least half the sins of mankind are caused by the fear of it."[3] Perhaps, if we dare to look this demon square in the eye, we may be able to tame it rather than destroy ourselves in futile attempts to escape. It is even remotely possible that if we sit quietly and meditate on the void that underlies our manic pursuits and distraction we may find that the monster we have feared for a lifetime is an angel in disguise. By tracing our way through the labyrinth of our dis-ease, we may find the path to health.

In the last century there was a common saying among doctors: "If you know syphilis, you know medicine" (because syphilis could manifest itself through such a wide variety of symptoms). The same might be said about boredom. Boredom is an element in all disease. Neurosis is boring yourself; psychosis is scaring yourself to death. Know your boredom, know yourself.

As we move more deeply into night country, into the heart of boredom, we will encounter all the major themes of psychology: guilt and shame, freedom and compulsion, will, imagination, feeling, sensation. By studying your boredom you may come to understand what motivates you, what values you hold, and what risks you must take to remain truly alive for all of your days.

The basic strategy this book suggests for dealing with boredom and the blues is: embrace them. Don't try positive thinking. A fundamental rule of the psyche is: *whatever you resist will persist.* Those who run from boredom and depression will spend a lifetime running. Surrender. Go into it. Study your dis-ease and it will lead you to health. Memorize your neurotic cycles and you

TURN AROUND AND FACE YOURSELF.

can run through them in minutes rather than weeks. Dealing with any "negative" emotion is like running the rapids in the Grand Canyon. In the turbulent Colorado River the greatest danger is getting thrown out of the boat and getting caught in a whirlpool or roller that sucks you down. If you struggle prematurely to get to the surface, you will likely drown. But if you go deeper, the action of the water will spit you out twenty feet downstream on the surface.

The philosophical and psychological view on which the diagnosis and prescriptions of this book are based is that boredom and depression are dis-eases by which the psyche is trying to heal itself. They are invitations to begin an inward-bound adventure, to descend into your depths and be reborn. The awareness of boredom is the gateway to the hero's journey. Pay attention and you may emerge more virile and wonder-ful. Blue is the color of melancholy and eternity. Go deep and find the wild blue yonder.

CHAPTER 2

A SHORT HISTORY OF THE BLUES
AND THE NOONTIDE DEMON

What is this silent dis-ease? What causes it? Can it be cured? Can we find our way out of gray boredom and black depression?

Before we can prescribe, we must describe. We have to be careful what words and concepts we use or we might fetch up the wrong treatment. If, for instance, we define boredom as a sin, as the early Christians did, we may have to discover a way to get divine forgiveness to cure it; if it is an impurity in the blood we might use leeches to suck out the bad blood; if it is an evil spirit we will need an exorcist; if it is pure monotony we may need a trip to Hawaii; if it is a chemical imbalance we may cure it with a pill.

The best way to begin is by standing back from our present condition. The ancestors of the modern experience of depression

WHOEVER NAMES THE DISEASE OWNS THE CURE.

and boredom are many: the "cast down" soul of the Psalms, the
black bile of Aristotle, the "demon of noontide" of the desert
monks, the *acedia* and *tristitia* (which Aquinas defines as the sorrow
and aversion we feel when we have acted against our own spiritual
good) of the medieval church, the melancholia of Hamlet, the
ennui of Pascal, the romantic *Weltschmerz* and *Langweile* of the
nineteenth century, the spleen of the English, the angst of
Kierkegaard, the nausea of Sartre. A hop, skip, and jump through
history will give us some perspective. How did peoples in other
times and places experience what we have come to call boredom?
How did they cure it?

Let's begin by trying to put ourselves in the skins of "primitive"
men and women. Mr. and Mrs. Flintstone sit by the entrance to
their cave. Both are very old and have not many years to live. He
is thirty-five, she thirty-two. She bore seven children (each birth
took enough calcium to cost her a tooth) but only two lived
beyond infancy. The cold that now makes their old joints arthritic
and the scarcity of food that makes each winter an ordeal were
too much for the little ones. Of the two that survived, one was
crippled by a rogue bear and walks with a bad limp. Still, they
have been lucky, or rather the gods have been good to them.
During most of their years game has been plentiful and the
winters short. This fall they are worried: the wild geese flew south
early and one terrifying evening the moon disappeared (eclipsed)
from a cloudless sky. The omens are strange.

As nearly as we can tell, they were never bored. In fact, they
lived near enough to the margin of terror—the unexpected
temper of wandering bears, marauding neighbors, and fickle

TERROR PUTS BOREDOM TO FLIGHT.

unseasonal storms—that they welcomed what little order, regularity, and monotony they could manage to introduce into their lives. Because their lives were so short and difficult, they never had time for midlife crises. (In some third-world countries the average life expectancy is still in the early forties.) Life was short, dramatic, and uncertain.

Consider how life expectancy affects modern people. By middle age, that is thirty-five to forty, we have completed a full round. We have been children, adolescents, full members of our tribe, gotten married, and had children. Our biological imperative has been fulfilled. We have "seen it all." But now we must start a second life, and that requires us to break out of the habits, roles, self-images, and jobs that have contained us during the first half. In threescore and ten there's time to be born, or bored, again and again.

But back to the Flintstones. On an early spring evening near the equinox, they and their neighbors gathered for a ceremony that was church, dance, feast, entertainment, and art all rolled into one. Every primitive tribe had some yearly cycle of ritual-story-dance to pay homage to the regularities of nature. (The idea of nature actually wasn't invented until late in human history, after machines had begun to change and pollute the garden.) Chants were repeated endlessly, magical formulas recited exactly as they had been recited by previous generations, the old myths were retold, the drums beat out a hypnotic rhythm. By endless repetition primitive peoples hoped to coerce the world into being orderly enough to give them the game and grain they needed to survive. Monotony was a triumph, not a terror. Order was celebrated by rites of passage.

LOVE IS ALWAYS WANTING TO DO IT AGAIN.

But within the tenuous order created by the web of myth-ritual-story that was spun over nature's uncontrollable wildness, the men and women who survived were those who could best improvise and react spontaneously to danger and opportunity. When the tiger burst into the circle of the campfire it immediately separated the quick from the dead. And people who did not know how to listen to their dreams and intuitions had no guidance. Survival depended on physical courage, endurance, the ability to withstand the hunger of lean winters and the pain of long marches.

By contrast, survival in the modern world depends on our ability to adapt ourselves to the monotonous (other names are "efficient," "orderly," "standardized") world created by the machine. A virtuous machine makes no mistake, creates no surprise, repeats itself, *ad infinitum, ad nauseam.* The virtues we produce are punctuality, dependability, predictability, and conformity to law and order.

Repetition, regularity, and orderliness, a triumph in former ages, have become the terror of modern times.

In the heyday of ancient Greece, monotony doesn't seem to have been much of a problem. There was no word for boredom. The Greeks knew the experience of satiation—desirelessness resulting from too much of a good thing—but nothing like the total state of depression and despair that finds a person fed up with all of life.

Two figures in Greek myths reflect an experience of futility. Sisyphus, for reasons not quite clear, is condemned by the gods to

WHEN NEW IS BORN, OLD DIES. CREATION ROOTS IN GRIEF, FLOWERS IN JOY.

an eternal life of rolling a boulder up a mountain only to have it roll back down just before he reaches the summit. He might well be the prototype for assembly-line workers who attach left rear fenders of Fords that are obsolete within a few years. And Tantalus is submerged up to his neck in water that recedes whenever he leans down to drink and is "tantalized" by a bunch of grapes overhead that vanishes when he reaches for it.

Aristotle does speak of a condition of melancholy very like the modern experience of depression. Four humors or bodily fluids, he says, mix in different proportions to create different types of people—blood, phlegm, yellow bile, and black bile. When the black bile predominates, a person is given to sorrow, disquietude, and unnameable sadness, and perhaps even to suicide. Troublesome as this temperament is, it is also the foundation of genius. Black bile may be a "sacred malady" that predisposes a man to creativity. Melancholy may be a hidden blessing.

Perhaps the nearest we get in the ancient world to modern boredom is among the Roman upper class. The poet Horace writes to his dissatisfied slave in charge of his country property and reminds him that when he was in the city he wanted to be in the country, and now that he is in the country he wants to be in the city. The only cure for such disquietude is hard physical labor. The Stoic philosopher Seneca complains of "taedium vitae," the tedium of life in which "the torpor of the soul [is] paralyzed in the midst of the ruins of its desires." (Here we have an almost exact replica of the modern experience—extreme boredom resulting from apathy, paralysis, and absence of desire.) His solution is to balance solitude and social life and to make a commitment to be involved in political affairs.

WHEN CHAOS IS KING WE WORSHIP ORDER. AND VICE VERSA.

Disgust with life was certainly momentarily experienced in the ancient world, but it never became a serious psychological or social problem. The ancient Greeks and the early Romans were animated by a buoyant and expansive feeling about life. The experiment of civilization was just beginning; reason was emerging and giving birth to the first fledgling science and to philosophy; democracy was in the bud. Men and women in this period of the adolescence of culture looked around them, saw the (divine) order in the movements of the stars, and hoped to bring such law and order into human affairs. They were possessed by a dream to make their cities as rational as the cosmos, and they worked to become cosmopolitan—citizens of a world governed by natural laws. In their youthful enthusiasm they took tragedy, failure, and even death in stride. In their eyes the world was still an arena for some rational-divine-orderly drama to be unfolded. When the blues visited them they lifted their eyes to the stars to be reminded that their small lives were contained within a cosmos that gave them meaning and purpose. Contemplation of the "starry skies above and the moral law within" (Kant) was sufficient to heal them of despondency.

Something happened to Greco-Roman buoyancy. A "failure of nerve," some have said. The reasons are complex and don't concern us here. What is important in our survey is that the feeling about life changed shortly before the beginning of the Christian era. It went from light to dark, from optimism to pessimism, from hope to despair, from confidence in the dream of earthly happiness to the conviction that human life was "fallen,"

ECOLOGY IS BELIEVING THE COSMOS HAS ITS LOGIC.

riddled with sin, and could be redeemed only by sacrificing present pleasure for future salvation. Gnosticism and Christianity introduced the first serious depression into Western culture, and the idea of acedia—a psychological or spiritual condition char- acterized by indifference, disgust, dryness, and torpor. Let's go into the desert where the earliest monks (the psychonauts, or spiritual explorers of an earlier time) were conducting their experiments in meditation, asceticism, and mysticism.

Nothing would satisfy Evagrius of Pontus (born A.D. 345) except the life of a solitary contemplative and monk. Although he was an archdeacon of Constantinople at an early age, he longed for the desert. Above all he wanted the hard path of the "athlete of God." When he was thirty-eight he left the bustling splendor of the center of the Eastern world (later Istanbul) to seek mystical union with God in the desert. After years of wrestling with God and the devil, he wrote a book on the eight capital sins in which he talks about acedia (from the Greek word meaning "lack of care"). From this we can reconstruct something of his experience.

Let's listen to his solitary thoughts: "Prayer and fasting are the only way. I must burn out every impulse to sin. Here on the desert the sun is both friend and enemy. It is my timepiece and my persecutor. I arise in the cool darkness, my mind and will bent toward God. I pray and wait. Evil thoughts creep into my mind. Sometimes I cannot help thinking of the moist cucumbers and yahouts and oranges I ate daily when I was in the city. Or the slave girl I passed in the market one day—naked to the waist, sweating, smelling of woman, slips into mind, haunts and troubles

IF LIFE IS HELL, A WISE MAN MAY CHOOSE TO DWELL IN A FOOL'S PARADISE.

me. Or pride attacks me, puffs me up and makes me think I am equal to Our Lord for the sufferings I undertake. When I have evil thoughts I discipline myself. No breakfast this morning, and if I cannot banish the visions of bathing in the cool waters of the Mediterranean I will deny myself my morning ration of water. Mortify the flesh: this is the only way to God. The pleasures of this life are vain and fleeting.

"During the morning hours my will remains constant, my spirit soars upward. There are times when the bliss is too great to be contained within my breast. God himself takes mercy on me and joins my spirit, as a bridegroom comes to the bride. For endless hours I am lost in eternal union. Bliss.

"But then toward midday 'the noontide demon' of which the Psalms speak assaults me. I fall as low into acedia as I have risen into the heavens. God seems to desert me, and I wonder why I am in this place. My spirit is dry, my faith vanishes, my will is weak as a hawk with a broken back. My mind casts up doubts—was my ecstasy of the morning real, or only a dream caused by a devil who drove me into this barren place? Why am I not back in Constantinople? The sadness overtakes me. Nothing I can do.

"Of all the vices, acedia is the worst. I can chastise my pride, replace my avarice with generosity, even quiet my concupiscence with the thought of my true desire for God. But acedia sucks my soul dry and leaves me no strength to fight back. This is the dark night of the soul. I know only this: when I endure it some depth is hollowed out in my soul that will later be filled by God. I am pushed down into this condition of sin to be raised up by the mercy of God. He must first make us nothing before he can bring us to Himself. So, I remain alone in this desert, waiting for the

WE ARE DRIVEN TO DISTRACTION TO ESCAPE CREEPING DESPAIR.

One who is Alone to take me to Himself. When I am finally nothing, God will come to me."

The ancient demon of noontide destroyed faith in an existing God. In the modern darkness of noon, all things sacred are in eclipse.

Jump over the Middle Ages (when acedia and sloth were defined as marks of sin to be erased only by diligent good works and the grace of God), and land in Elizabethan England.

Shakespeare, whose characters represent an encyclopedia of human virtues and vices, gives us a portrait of boredom incarnate in Hamlet. The melancholy Dane makes a career of mourning, indecision, and world-weariness. "How weary, stale, flat, and unprofitable seem to me all the uses of this world."

Listen to his description of the inner world of melancholy:

I have of late—but wherefore I know not—lost all my mirth, forgone all custom of exercises; and indeed it goes so heavily with my disposition that this goodly frame, the earth, seems to me a sterile promontory; this most excellent canopy, the air, look you, this brave o'erhanging firmament, this majestical roof fretted with golden fire, why, it appears no other thing to me but a foul and pestilent congregation of vapours. What a piece of work is man! how noble in reason! how infinite in faculty! in form and moving how express and admirable! in action how like an angel! in apprehension how like a god! the beauty of the world! the paragon of animals! And yet, to me, what is this quintessence of dust? man delights not me. . . .

IN ALIEN NATIONS THE EXILE DISCOVERS THE MEANING OF HOME.

The world lies shimmeringly beautiful before Hamlet, yet he is exiled from it. Delight has turned to disgust. Stripped of all nobility and meaning, Hamlet is unable to act. He is caught in the impotent contemplation of suicide—"to be or not to be, that is the question." And like many a modern antihero, his only action is to strike out in blind violence, to kill what he is unable to love.

Pascal (1623–1662) takes the sense of being exiled from a potentially delightful life as characteristic of the entire human condition and becomes the philosopher of ennui. Here we see emerging the first hints of the modern, existentialist view of the person caught between boredom and terror.

Pascal was a troubled genius. By the age of twelve he had worked out Euclid's propositions for himself; by nineteen he had invented a calculating machine; by twenty-two he had formulated an important scientific theory of the vacuum. At an early age he moved among an elite circle of French intellectuals. All of this he rejected for voluntary poverty and severe asceticism before his death at thirty-nine.

In his view, man is a creature of extremes, a beast and a fallen angel. We are haunted on one side by the beauty of the Garden of Eden from which we have been exiled and on the other by the terrifying infinite spaces of the universe. The following is from his *Pensées*:

> When I consider the short extent of my life, swallowed in eternity before and after, the small space that I fill or even see, engulfed in the infinite immensity of spaces unknown to

THE MACHINE AUGURS A BORING FUTURE.

me and which know me not, I am terrified and astounded to
find myself here and not there. For there is no reason why
it should be here, not there, why now rather than at another
time. Who put me here? By whose order and design have
this place and time been allotted to me? The memory of a
guest that tarrieth for a day.

To escape the horror and disappointment of existence, human
beings will run in any direction. At all costs we flee from the
specter of death and the hopelessness of life without God. For the
average person life becomes a constant search for entertainment
and diversion—a vain flight from ennui, because of "the natural
evil of our weak and mortal condition, which is so wretched that
once we dwell on it nothing can console us." (*Pensées*, 205)
Gambling, the company of women, high office, theater, riding to
the hounds—all of these amusements serve only to keep us from
thinking about our unhappy condition. If, by chance, we struggle
to succeed and win for ourselves the conditions that would
make for a secure and contented life, we are doubly in
danger because then we must face our terror. As long as we can
get caught up in the excitement of the chase, we can forget
ourselves. Striving for success is ultimately better than achieving
it.

201. Boredom (ennui). A man finds nothing so unbearable
as to be completely idle, without passions, occupations,
amusements, or reading. Then he feels that he is nothing:
lonely, inadequate, dependent, powerless, and empty. And
immediately there spring from deep in his heart boredom,
gloom, sadness, vexation, anger, and despair. . . .

MAN CREATED MACHINE IN HIS IMAGE. AND IT RETURNED THE FAVOR.

Although "all men's misfortunes spring from the single cause that they are unable to stay quietly in one room," quiet and meditation are no solutions to the threat of boredom. Introspection or the inner search is no more likely to yield happiness than blind grasping after amusements. Mankind is a creature of boredom. We are condemned to be bored or, worse, to spend a lifetime running from it.

Like most mystics, Pascal finds the cure in the dis-ease. Boredom is a blessing in disguise; it is a bridge across the void of this world to God. "The greatness of man lies in his knowledge that he is miserable. Once we recognize our inner emptiness a vacuum is created into which God can come. This infinite abyss can be filled only by an infinite and immutable object, that is to say, by God." To discover that happiness which is our birthright and from which we have been exiled, we must first be stripped of all pretensions and evasions. We must confront our mortality.

In his emphasis on life in the amusement park as a way of trying to evade boredom, Pascal sounds very modern. But his solution to the problem—waiting for the void to be filled by the grace of God—marks him as still living in a world of belief. God had not yet died; hence he could come in at the last moment—a deus ex machina—and save man from the worst. It is precisely the loss of this faith that a transcendent God can intervene to rescue us from death and nothingness that makes modern boredom so much more desperate than anything Pascal or the Christian mystics experienced.

The modern variety of boredom arose in the nineteenth century. Previously, men and women suffered from black bile,

---

ABSTRACTION IS A THIEF THAT STEALS FROM THE CONCRETE. (APHORISM IS A LIAR.)

acedia, and melancholy but not boredom. Wives got tired of grinding corn and chasing kids and waking up to the same face every morning, but they were not bored. An Egyptian slave on the assembly crew for the pyramids felt the futility of moving blocks to make a giant triangle in the desert but was not bored. We can assume this because experience is connected to language and the word *boredom* only came into use a little more than a century ago.

If we pay close attention to the images and connotations that sleep in the word we will discover the key to the modern experience.

bore: to pierce especially by means of a rotary tool, as a drill or auger

bore: to afflict with ennui: depress, weary, and annoy by dullness: crush with irksome tediousness

Boredom sprung suddenly into the English vocabulary. As nearly as scholars can tell, it was not originally associated with any of the other words used to characterize similar experiences. The image is taken from the world of machines: a bit goes round and round, biting ever deeper until it wears a hole in the substance being bored.

Modern boredom is not like water dripping on a rock; it is like a machine grinding us down.

A major cause, perhaps *the* major cause, of boredom is that we have become machine-minded. Just as technology shaped our outside world, it has also given us the images we use to understand ourselves. The modern myth is *Frankenstein*. We created a monster that threatens to destroy us. It is an oversimplification, but in broad outline the history of the modern world could be summarized in three statements:

The machine was invented. (Man took over.)
God died. (Nature was desecrated.)
Humans were bored. (To death? Perhaps!)

Let's trace the logic of events that gave rise to the modern problem of boredom.

The machine was invented. With steam engines, gasoline engines, mass-produced Model T Fords, Caterpillar tractors, airplanes, human beings took over the planet, seized control of the direction of evolution. The machine shrunk time and space and concentrated power and population. People poured into cities, broke their connection with the rhythms of the seasons and the habit of planting-waiting-hoping-harvesting. Nature became a "thing," raw material to be fabricated into objects that promised happiness and wealth. A man's worth came to be measured by abstract tokens—money—rather than by land, cattle, family, personal power, and stories. The further we have moved from farming, hunting, and gathering, the more our lives have been speeded up. The cadence of modern life is the unbroken intensity of machines. Bertrand Russell puts it well:

Whatever we may wish to think we are creatures of Earth. . . . The rhythm of Earth life is slow; autumn and

WHAT'S GOOD FOR THE EARTH IS NOT GENERAL MOTORS' BUSINESS.

winter are as essential to it as spring and summer, and rest is as essential as motion. . . . It is necessary to preserve some contact with the ebb and flow of terrestrial life. . . . For all these reasons a generation that cannot endure boredom will be a generation of little men, of men unduly divorced from the slow process of nature, of men in whom every vital impulse slowly withers as though they were cut flowers in a vase.[1]

"Cut flowers in a vase." What are we cut off from? Nature, certainly. More than that, the cosmos as a created order in which a divine drama was being played.

In a brilliant book on the history of ennui, *The Demon of Noontide*, Reinhard Kuhn characterizes the difference between the ancient and modern experiences of boredom:

Previously, certain values had always existed and ennui resulted from the inability to live up to these generally accepted values. The belief in such unattainable, and yet existing, truths made it possible for even pessimists to dream of sainthood. That option has now been closed, and all that is left is the anguish that comes from no longer being able to find any values.[2]

Until modern times people had always lived within an over-arching scheme of meaning; God or the gods were experienced as working within the natural order of things. The yearly harvest was the visible proof of the bounty of the gods. All that was changed by the machine. We became aliens in our own world.

COMPULSION SWALLOWED THE CLOCK. CELEBRATION SPIT IT OUT.

The forests and wild places became terrifying and strange. (To the woods, to the woods, the villain says. No. No. Anything but the woods, the heroine replies.) The only intimate God we ever knew, the sanctity homogenized into the world surrounding us, was killed by the machine.

No one has captured this experience of the death of nature's god better than Sartre. In *Nausea*, the antihero Antoine Roquentin describes his feeling about nature as a sticky marmalade when he looks at a garden:

> Had I dreamed of this enormous presence? It was there, in the garden, toppled down into the trees, all soft, sticky, soiling everything, all thick, a marmalade. And I was inside, I with the garden. I was frightened, furious, I thought it was so stupid, so out of place, I hated this ignoble mess. . . . I was not surprised, I knew it was the World, the naked World suddenly revealing itself, and I choked with rage at this gross, absurd being. You couldn't even wonder where all that sprang from or how it was that a world came into existence, rather than nothingness. . . . I shouted, "Filth! What a rotten filth!" and I shook myself to get rid of this sticky filth, but it held fast and there was so much, tons and tons of existence, endless: I stifled at the depths of this immense weariness. . . . I felt with boredom that I had no way of understanding.

Faced with a desacralized nature (now nauseating and meaningless), modern man has tried to become the missing god. If value and meaning are absent in our world, then we will

---

WHAT PACE ON EARTH MAKES GOODWILL TOWARD MEN AND WOMEN, SLOTHS, JAGUARS, AND WHALES?

manufacture them. The heroes in Sartre's novels are typical. They begin in despair because nothing of value can be discovered. Their only salvation is to create. The only escape from boredom is to face the nothingness and terror of life and create a meaning for your personal life in the face of the void. But unfortunately our image of creation comes from the way machines produce rather than the way corn grows. Hence, to create meaning for our lives we fall into machine-mindedness.

Modern boredom is the symptom of our successful failure. We have interiorized the machine. We have come to expect of ourselves the same kind of regularity, efficiency, interchangeability, and feelinglessness as we do from our machines. We live compulsively, moving to the regular measure of clock time rather than taking our own time. (The Greeks had two words for time: *chronos* was measured clock time; *kairos* was organic time.) We expect to work an eight-hour day, forty-hour week until we are obsolete, i.e., "retired" at sixty-five.

We measure our worth by productivity, output. Imagination and feeling must be kept under strict control. No daydreaming on the job! At the end of the day we go "home" to pigeonhole apartments or numbered houses in tic-tac-toe suburbs. Most recently, even the intimate part of our being has fallen prey to machines. The heart is a pump that might be replaced by a plastic device; the mind is only a complex computer.

The science fiction stories in which the machines rebel and take over—*Demon Seed*—are a mirror not of the future but of the present. The imperative of the machine is forcing us to march to its cadences. We must have full production. Our machines must be kept busy. Otherwise our economy will lag. No matter that our cancerous rate of industrial growth is threatening to pollute us

CONSUMERS LACK A CONSUMING PASSION.

into oblivion, to destroy the sacred earth. Charlie Chaplin showed us in *Modern Times* how we are caught in the machine. Round and round we go. It bores deeper until it wears a hole in our soul; our enthusiasm leaks out and leaves us empty and depressed.

A complete analysis of the causes of modern boredom is complex. We will unravel many of the interrelated strands as we go deeper into diagnosis and prescription. In the technological world families are broken up regularly (the average American moves every five years), and community disappears. With rootlessness goes anomie—normlessness. Entertainment, the quest for excitement, replaces deep satisfaction. We buy and consume to fill the emptiness and give us a sense of worth. In back of these complex causes lies the tyranny of the machine and machine values from which we need to be freed, so we may once again move at a pace that will allow us to savor our feelings, to listen to our dreams.

I remember vividly the summer of 1958. I was working the three-to-eleven shift at Electric Hose and Rubber Company in Wilmington, Delaware. God, it was awful! Hot, noisy, and boring. For eight hours I repeated the same set of motions. My job was to roll plastic garden hose into a tight circle—round and round, 17½ revolutions per hose—put on the end couplings, tie it, and put the finished product in a box. The unofficial daily quota was 200 hoses. By working hard I could easily do this number in five hours, but I dared not. "Don't up the quota" was the rule. There was no incentive paid for extra productivity.

I tried everything to make the job interesting. I tried to

PROPHETS DON'T SOAR ON COMPANY TIME.

daydream, but after a couple of hours my mind was lulled into a blank. The job required just enough attention to prevent any creative thinking. Finally, I hit on something mildly interesting. I tore pages from a German grammar and memorized vocabulary and verb forms. But one day the boss caught me talking out loud to myself and said there was to be no learning on company time. The hours crept by. I found myself looking forward to lunch. I began smoking, because smokers were allowed a fifteen-minute break in early evening. The summer seemed years long.

Each Friday night at eleven freedom arrived. My wife picked me up at the plant and we drove the 100 miles to Bethany Beach. We pitched a small tent on the dunes. In the early hours of the morning I plunged into the ink-black sea and let wave after wave wash over me until I was cleansed from the week and the smell of rubber was washed away. Finally, just before dawn, we would make love and go to sleep until the sun drove us from our tent. Then, for hours, we lay on white sand, baptized ourselves in the jade water, and filled our eyes with the endless blue sky. Only then did my mind spring back to life and my spirit revive.

As we moved in a single lifetime from simple to complex machines, we have moved from optimism to depression. Our experience is reflected in our language and song. We have seen the evolution of the blues, a change in the quality and meaning of the experience of melancholy.

In the 1930s, Americans sang the blues ("I got the weary, lonesome, homesick blues"). We had the blues in the night and the lovesick blues. In those days "blue" meant longing and nostalgia, the sense that life was frequently lonely and sometimes

THE ANTIDOTE FOR BOREDOM IS NOT FOR SALE.

left us dry, and wanting more. We weren't affluent then. Everybody was poor and about half empty. It was all right to be blue, because we were on the road to somewhere. Maybe California. The future still looked promising.

With the second great war, the blues retreated for a while. American sacrifice would make the world safe for democracy; there would be no more depressions. But in 1945 we began to live under the mushroom cloud. A permanent shadow of despair loomed over us. Between Korea and Vietnam we lost our innocence and gained our affluence. We arrived. We were number one in power and production, and proud of it. It was only a matter of time before the War on Poverty would wipe out the last pockets of peril.

In the meantime the credit card society had proclaimed an end to delayed gratification. No more waiting, planning, and working for distant rewards. *Paradise Now!* In the process of claiming the new right to instant satisfaction, we hardly noticed that we were losing our capacity to dream, to hope, to sacrifice, to be excited by anticipation.

Advertising and manufacturing made it a crime to be hungry, empty. They promised us that every longing could be filled by some product. Of course, it wasn't. We became ashamed of our emptiness, our cosmic nostalgia. The blues stopped being a gentle melancholy, a plaintive and tender lament about the essential incompleteness of life. The blues became an ugly, shameful restlessness, a psychological problem, a sign of neurosis and maladjustment, a disease called depression.

CHAPTER 3

LIFE-STYLES: RUNNERS, FIGHTERS, AND HIDERS

To understand why some people spend a lifetime running from boredom and others embrace it, we must begin with the fact that life in the raw is equally frightening and exciting. Under the facade of business-as-usual and "of course I'll meet you tomorrow for lunch" lurks a void of unpredictability. Our lives are always in danger.

In the animal world there are different styles of dealing with danger: there are runners, fighters, and hiders; deer, gorillas, and possums. When a deer spots a mountain lion, its body is instantly prepared to do what is necessary to survive: blood pressure and heart rate are accelerated, bowels are emptied. It runs from the

LIVE DANGEROUSLY! OR NOT AT ALL.

danger. When a gorilla spots an invading enemy, it puffs its chest, drums, makes fierce displays, and prepares to fight—if necessary. When a possum senses danger, it freezes, plays dead, and hopes the danger will disappear.

In the human world we can see the same patterns of response.

Runners and fighters (what Drs. Friedman and Rosenman in *Type A Behavior and Your Heart* refer to as Type A personalities) are always prepared for dealing with danger. Their sympathetic-adrenal systems are constantly in an overactive condition, in a state of red alert. They are always on the move, scanning the horizon for enemies.

A majority of Americans fall into this category. We are by national temperament and training competitors. We are out to be the biggest, the best, the winners. We are a "can do" people. We are intensity freaks; we want something always to be happening. Keeping busy is our major way of dealing with life. The American male, in particular, is always in a hurry. Our chief personality style is the extroverted activist.

Hiders, or Type B personalities, try to blend into the environment like camouflaged animals and remain quiet and stay out of harm's way. Their response to danger involves a predominant use of the vagal-parasympathetic systems. In the presence of danger their blood pressure drops, their pulse rate slows down. They try to conceal themselves by freezing in place, remaining passive. This pattern of response is more common among women than men in American culture. Traditionally, women were expected to remain in the background, be yielding, silent, unobtrusive, charmingly helpless. Aggressive women were said to be "castrating" or behaving "just like a man." In cultures such as the Hopi or Navajo,

IF YOU "HAVE NEVER BEEN BORED A DAY IN YOUR LIFE," YOU HAVE BEEN RUNNING FROM SOMETHING.

this softer Type B personality is the norm and is valued over the aggressive stance toward life.

Type A personalities run from (or try to conquer) boredom. If you ask them, they will frequently deny that they have ever been bored. If we look only superficially, we may take them at their word. But when we see the price they pay for remaining constantly in motion, we discover that their lives are shaped by a compulsive effort to escape from boredom. The stress flowing from unbroken intensity and competition is *the* major factor in heart attacks and possibly in cancer. The cost of pushing (besides hemorrhoids) is exhaustion, or what was once called "nervous breakdowns."

In running from boredom, Type A persons fall into the swamp of fatigue or worse. They escape the minor dis-ease of boredom by repressing and keeping it unconscious, only to fall prey to something far more serious—depression or despair. Since our most popular personality style in America is manic, our most common psychological malady is depression.

Lance is a 100 percent man. The sort who reads *Playboy*, owns his own manufacturing company, is financially secure (with a lot of help from borrowed capital), and is always busy. At fifty he is still lean, wiry, handsome, and boyish in appearance. He drives a Corvette, never less than 75 mph, and flies his own airplane. When he is not working he plays with the same intensity that made him an early success. On any weekend he might be hang gliding, skin diving along the New Jersey coast, or flying with his latest woman friend to Bermuda.

YOU ARE CAUGHT BY WHAT YOU ARE RUNNING FROM.

In the years I have known Lance I have never seen him bored. On the surface he seems to have escaped ennui. But look deeper. Follow him around for a week and you'll find he never sits still for more than fifteen minutes without fidgeting. His mind is always racing. He seems perpetually to be in two places at once. On the rare occasions when his children (from a marriage that broke up two years ago) visit for a few days, he seems distracted and irritated. The children behave like little adults. No horseplay. No noise. No hilarious giggling. Every two or three months Lance's energy drains out of him, like water from a tub, and he looks gray. For two or three weeks he acts like a robot. No feeling, no enthusiasm, no reason for being alive. During these times he redoubles his efforts at work. His voice becomes clipped. He worries about the company's stock and the business climate. Even during the best of times he seldom relaxes. I have never heard him laugh from deep in his belly.

Type B personalities are boredom-prone rather than boredom-escapers. Their encounter with boredom is on a conscious rather than an unconscious level. They usually admit they're sometimes bored but not often depressed. They tolerate boredom much better than anxiety and aggression, and are not threatened by inactivity or lack of intensity.

Ellen is fortyish, raven-haired and lively. A late starter. After a stint as a *Time* researcher and a season in the Peace Corps, she decided she wanted to become a therapist and flew through graduate school in record time. There is something of the waif in

A FUGITIVE IS A PRISONER IN MOTION.

her look—a touch of sadness in her eyes, a hint of homelessness, a fear of abandonment left over from too many years in foster homes. Yet her face can break out of darkness quick as lightning flashes across a south Florida storm front.

When I first met her she was getting over a three-year romance. The trauma had drawn her thin. I asked her if she was ever bored. "I don't think so," she replied. "But I'm not afraid of it. When I get very sad I just go to sleep. I could be alone all weekend and just sleep. I guess it's because I'm an introvert. If you're an introvert you aren't dependent so much on the outside world. You always carry around your own richness, your fantasies, your imagination. When I sleep, I dream, so I'm not afraid of the dark side of life. I suppose that sometimes I am bored. But I don't mind it. There are times in my life when very little is happening, and this is okay with me. In fact, I need the fallowness to rest and catch up with myself. I need relief from intensity. Living alone, I get lonely a lot more than I get bored."

So there are two major styles in dealing with boredom:

Runners and Warriors	*Hiders*
Type A personalities	Type B personalities
Live with high degree of aggression, anxiety, activity and stress, and low tolerance for boredom.	Live more passively or responsively with little stress or intensity and have a higher tolerance for boredom.
Tendency toward mania.	Tendency toward depression.
Extroverts.	Introverts.

YOU ARE NEVER OLD UNTIL YOU START RETIRING.

Tend to break through barriers, make decisions, take action, incur guilt. Their dis-ease springs from their constant doing.

Tend to remain within comfortable limits and avoid being outstanding. More likely to suffer shame for their failure to risk definitive action. Their dis-ease springs from the vacuum— what they have not done.

They try always to be optimistic, stay on the sunny side, think positively.

They are more accustomed to the ups and downs, are acquainted with the blues in the night and the dark nights of the soul.

No matter which is your style, you will need to find a way of dealing with danger and boredom. Avoidance of the darker side of experience forces boredom underground, where it then erupts as violence, depression, or disease.

Since there is no avoiding it, let's go deeper until we feel at home with blue Mondays and black moods.

CHAPTER 4

A MAP FOR PSYCHONAUTS

Are you bored? Or just tired? Or lonely? Or depressed?

How near are you to despair? Are you more angry or apathetic? Exactly what do you feel?

Surprisingly, a majority of people cannot give exact answers to these questions. Most of us are not experts either at identifying or dealing with our own emotions. We frequently mistake or repress awareness of our most intimate responses to other people and situations. You may be angry, bored, or depressed without knowing it. But your body will always register what you feel. If you habitually feel but do not acknowledge resentment, an ulcer or other psychosomatic symptom will appear as a substitute way of expressing your anger. Have you noticed how often, when you

---

YOUR BEST-KEPT SECRETS ARE THOSE YOU KEEP FROM YOURSELF.

have a miserable cold, you remember you were silently angry at your husband or depressed about your work for days before you came down with the cold?

The "negative" feelings that range from boredom to despair are particularly difficult to identify clearly. As we go deeper into night country, it gets increasingly darker. In simple boredom we become lethargic and dull, lulled to sleep by the monotony of our situation. In chronic boredom and depression we descend into agitated confusion and further paralysis of awareness and will. Something is wrong. But what is it?

By the time we drop into despair and edge toward suicide, we are shut down. We can't remember what made us happy, or how we found the courage to make decisions, or what made life worth living. Obscurity, confusion, self-encapsulation, the gradual closing in of our horizons—these are the defining characteristics of the "descent into hell." The "pit and the pendulum," the walls close in on us.

To move away from your dis-ease, you must first find out where you are. The healing process begins when you identify the feeling of discomfort and name the dis-ease. In many primitive tribes the shaman (those early psychotherapists whom we disparagingly call witch doctors) who was called on to cure a sick person would go into a trance, travel to the "underworld," and discover the name of the evil spirit or demon that was troubling the sufferer. Knowing the name gave the shaman power over the demons. Our modern equivalent is the inward-bound journey, plunging into the chaos of our unconscious, clarifying our feelings, and gaining in-sight. By shining the light of awareness into our inner world—introspection—we illuminate the night country so we can travel there without undue fear. We free

To be whole re/member your parts.

ourselves from tiresome efforts to maintain an artificial level of intensity so we can escape boredom, as well as the threat that depression will descend on us and turn us into victims.

Before we can look closely at the elements that make up the experience of boredom, we have to locate it in relation to other dark feelings: fatigue, monotony, chronic boredom, depression, despair, apathy, suicide. We need a map of the "negative," passive emotions that lead us deeper into darkness and captivity.

Imagine that the road into the night country begins in a wide circle and gradually spirals downward. Each revolution of the road takes us a stage deeper into the pit of despair, where it appears that suicide is the only way out. As the circles tighten, our horizons shrink. We become more constricted, more compulsive. Imagination, feeling, thinking, sensation, will—all the faculties of the personality—are increasingly weak and circumscribed. The person who keeps circling downward becomes gradually more self-encapsulated, rigid, alienated, self-obsessed. Someone caught in this downward spiral resembles the mythical Suicircle bird that was said to fly at ever-increasing speeds in ever-diminishing circles until it finally flew up its own ass and died.

Let's carry the analogy of a map of emotions a step further. If we can chart the "negative" emotions and make a map of night country, we should be able to trace the outlines of the "positive" emotions.

Maps are useful only if you want to take a journey. Philosophy and religion alike have pictured the authentic life as a heroic journey into the depths and heights, the descent into hell, the ascent of the holy mountain. In the old days, when every tribe had a revealed religion and authoritative books and priests, the maps for life were given each child—the Ten Command-

---

PSYCHONAUTS NEED MAPS OF INNER SPACE.

ments and the Law of Moses, the Sermon on the Mount, the Eightfold Path of Buddhism. In the twentieth century, these traditional religious maps are being questioned. There is widespread doubt and confusion. But without a map we lose the confidence that life is a journey that has a point, a goal, or a purpose. We wander aimlessly, lost in the wilderness of confusing experiences. New gurus and political messiahs step in and give the most desperate something to believe in. Marx, Hitler, Castro, Jim Jones, Saddam Hussein, Reverend Moon—all offer us official maps. Which of them can we trust?

Why not begin with yourself? With your own emotions, thoughts, intuitions, sensations? What is the meaning and purpose of your life? What should you do?

Nature-God-Life intends something through you. You are a part of an evolving, cosmic adventure. The most direct and trustworthy place to find how you may fit into the overall scheme of things is your own experience. Your emotions will provide you with a compass to guide you on your journey. Discovering the path that will lead you toward a meaningful and rich life is something like the game we played as children: someone hid something and when we went to hunt for it they gave us clues—"You're getting warmer. Now you're getting colder." The overarching meaning of life remains a mystery. It will always be hidden. But we can tell when we are getting closer or farther away from our own individual paths into the heart of the mystery by consulting our own feelings and dreams.

Once we have a map of the emotions, any emotion can serve as a compass by which we may find our location. Here we will focus on boredom, because it is a biological warning signal, direct feedback from the cosmos and your inner guidance system, that

NATURE GAVE YOU A COMPASS FOR YOUR JOURNEY.

something you are doing is not right for you. When you begin to yawn and turn to lead, you have immediate evidence that you are not engaged, interested, employed. Your potential is not being used. The promise of your life is being broken.

Boredom is a gentle signal. Nature gets your attention by the slightly painful agitation caused by listlessness. If you don't respond to the first signal, stronger ones will follow—depression, pain, mild illness, despair, life-threatening illness, and (if you are a very poor listener) perhaps premature death. If you become an expert at identifying and dealing with boredom, you can correct your course through life before you have gone seriously astray. Think of boredom as a biocosmic beeper, alerting you that something more engaging awaits if you have the courage to move out of the swamp where your journey has become bogged down.

To examine boredom and its immediate psychological neighbors; we need to sketch a very rough map of both the downward spiraling road into night country and the ascent spiral toward the light. Remember that maps and metaphors can be misleading. The fluid and always miraculous psyche is not bound to walk in straight lines. It can hop, skip, and jump from despair to joy in a moment, although the map places them far apart. With due precautions, I offer this life map. Warning! Any map or metaphor taken literally is hazardous to your spiritual health.

BOREDOM MEANS YOU ARE SLIGHTLY OFF COURSE.

Wonder—Joy

Communion, Compassion, Service

Risking and Acting

Renewal of Desire

Imagination and Dreams

Renewal of Feeling—Pain and Pleasure

Mindfulness—Doing Nothing

Guilt and Shame Barrier

Upward path toward ease, health, increasing engagement, consciousness, communion, aliveness, freedom, response/ability—an open universe.

Compulsion—Drivenness

Fatigue

Monotony

Chronic Boredom

Depression

Despair

Apathy

Victim Stance

Illness

Suicide

Downward path toward dis-ease, increasing isolation, anomie, deadness, meaninglessness, drivenness—a closed horizon.

THE MAP FOR THE ASCENT TO HEAVEN APPEARS ON THE REVERSE SIDE OF THE MAP FOR THE DESCENT INTO HELL.

CHAPTER 5

FATIGUE: THE PERSONAL ENERGY CRISIS

The energy crisis has hit you. You always seem to be tired and irritable. Nothing is quite right. You don't have as much energy as you once did. You're frequently tired without apparent reason. Maybe you're just getting old. Sometimes you feel more worn out when you get up in the morning than when you went to bed; the very thought of going to work makes you slightly sick at your stomach. (*Should I call in sick?*) Even the weekends and the yearly vacation don't refresh you at a deep level. You can still muddle through, but you don't have much enthusiasm for your family, your work, or even your hobbies. One day just seems to follow another. Tedious.

If you're tired, run-down, washed out, and Geritol doesn't make

IF YOU DON'T SLOW UP, YOU'LL GET RUN-DOWN.

you sparkle, if your future looks as exciting as oatmeal without cream or brown sugar, welcome to the club. You suffer from the most common of all medical complaints—*lingering fatigue*. And your doctor probably can't cure you.

Why? What's wrong? What are the causes of fatigue?

Let's begin with the number one cause. A majority of the world's fatigue is caused by malnutrition, not enough (or the right kind of) food. Four hundred and fifty-five million people in the world are malnourished or face starvation yearly because they do not have enough food. The World Food Council says that last year alone 16 million children under five died from malnutrition or diseases to which they were made vulnerable by malnutrition. In many underprivileged countries vast segments of the population suffer from irreversible brain damage and perpetual fatigue due to malnutrition. Unless you are one of the very few deprived Americans, this is not immediately relevant to your problem of fatigue. But it is good to keep the problem of fatigue in America and other wealthy nations in perspective.

While we are on disagreeable subjects, we may as well dispose of the second major cause of fatigue—serious illness. After a few months of unexplained weariness, most of us suspect the worst. The fatigue may be the first symptom of an undiagnosed disease— mononucleosis, chronic fatigue syndrome, hepatitis, heart disease, diabetes, or—to imagine the worst—cancer. And it could be. Fatigue *is* a major component of most serious diseases, and you can't rule out the worst possibilities without a thorough medical examination. So (to repeat the advice given *ad nauseam* to protect Dear Abby and other advice givers from malpractice suits) get a checkup.

But before you do, don't get too anxious. Chances are four out of five that your doctor won't find much wrong with you.

FILL IN THE BLANK: "I'M SICK AND TIRED OF ————."

Dr. F. N. Allan reported that in studying 300 cases in which the chief complaint was fatigue or weakness, he found that physical disorders accounted for only 20 percent of the cases. The rest he attributed to "nervous conditions."[1]

Fatigue is so persistent and elusive that doctors in every age have had their favorite diagnosis and prescriptions. For dark humors and bad blood, use eye of newt and leeches. When possessed by sloth—the devil's chief agent—pray to God to strengthen your will and make you industrious. In the nineteenth century, when medicine was in a flush of excitement over scientific method and considered the body an intricate machine, fatigue was diagnosed as neurasthenia, or nervous exhaustion. This diagnosis sometimes led to radical surgery to cure fatigue. As late as 1932, Dr. G. Crile removed the nerves from the adrenal glands of patients with "neurocirculatory asthenia." The operation was based on the assumption that surgical steps were needed to reduce the stimulation of the adrenal-sympathetic system in patients whose mental and psychic mechanism was normal but whose sympathetic nervous system was chronically overstimulated.

Modern physicians and psychologists have engaged in the usual mind-body debates about the primary cause of fatigue. Those who prefer physical causes find the culprit in either the cells or the glands. Psychologists generally believe the problem is rooted in emotional conflicts and lack of psychological harmony. Most recently, holistic health practitioners have indicted our dietary habits and our sedentary ways of life.

No doubt everyone in this debate is right. Mind, body, emotion, environment—all contribute to fatigue. A human being

MEDICINE IS THE PRACTICE OF PHILOSOPHY WITHOUT A LICENSE. AND VICE VERSA.

is a psychosomatic-spiritual-social entity. Anything we do affects everything else. When we eat poorly our biochemistry is not optimum and this affects our moods, which affect our action, which affects our feedback, which affects our moods, *ad infinitum.* In fact, no one is smart enough to assign an exact percentage of causation to the various factors that contribute to fatigue. Causes also differ for different people.

To get some handle on the problem, let's invent some statistics. Let's speculate that 21 percent of your fatigue (provided you are among the 80 percent that has no serious disease) is due to poor diet. As a generalization, Americans are sugar and fat junkies, and that tends to speed us up at the same time as it weighs us down. Our dominant nutritional problem is overeating. We would all be healthier and have more energy if we ate a diet rich in raw fruits, vegetables, and complex carbohydrates and lowered our sugar and fat consumption.

An additional 29 percent of chronic fatigue is possibly due to lack of strenuous exercise. Twenty million joggers have recently discovered that running lessens anxiety, increases energy, dispels depression, and increases the sense of resolve and well-being. When middle-aged men begin a program of jogging, they become more emotionally stable, calm, self-sufficient, and imaginative.

Moving is good for the emotions. So good, in fact, that Dr. Paavo Airola, a noted health-food advocate, says: "If you have to make a choice between eating junk food and exercising strenuously or eating health food and not exercising at all, it is better to eat the junk food and exercise." Diet and exercise are a lot better for increasing energy than pep pills. Caffeine, amphetamines, and sugar

EVERY PRESCRIPTION CONTAINS A HIDDEN ASSUMPTION.

are immediate stimulants, but they eventually exhaust the nervous system.

Still, diet and exercise combined only raise your energy quotient by 50 percent. The largest determinant of personal energy is attitude, self-image, the sense of the worth of one's labor and life. In the most extreme conditions in concentration camps, some individuals maintained the energy and will to live because of their beliefs. Someone who is highly motivated may expend massive energy without feeling fatigue. Some forms of stress release more energy than they consume. Artists in a burst of creativity may paint or write for days with little sleep or food.

The two most effective antidotes for lingering fatigue are fascination and purposefulness. A high degree of choice, concentration, and enjoyment of a lifework is necessary to keep energy at a high level. Constant stimulation, whether by drugs, entertainment, or excitement without interest or fascination, in the long run, increases rather than alleviates fatigue. We are seldom too tired to do what we really want to do.

In recent years a new medical catchall has been used to explain disease—stress. Dr. Hans Selye discovered and popularized the notion that stress is the all-purpose culprit. When animals perceive some threat, their flight-fight mechanisms are activated. But in the modern world the dangers that threaten the human animal are so nebulous and ever-present—economic disaster, nuclear war, environmental disintegration, loss of social status— that many people have the emergency switch stuck in the "on" position most of the time. This constant stimulation of the adrenal-sympathetic system produces emotional and physical fatigue; if ignored, it leads to disease.

ANY THING IS LINKED TO EVERY THING. A SINGLE FACT IS ALWAYS MARRIED.

The concept of stress is elegant and useful because it undercuts many false problems. Stress may come from any number of sources—poor diet, family conflict, unresolved anger, noise, monotony, or merely too much excitement. Along with fatigue and disease, it is always caused by an interaction involving body, mind, spirit, and environment.

The much-publicized Holmes-Rahe Social Readjustment Rating Scale[2] gives us an interesting perspective on stress and fatigue:

THE SOCIAL READJUSTMENT RATING SCALE

To use the Social Readjustment Scale, check off events that have happened to you within the last year, then add up the total number of stress units. Use the blank lines between items to add your own life-stress events, and assign the appropriate number of points by comparing it to the events ranked in the chart.

This so-called Holmes-Rahe Social Readjustment Scale found that a score of 150 for events occurring within the last year gives you a 50–50 chance of developing an illness. A score of 300 + gives you an 80 percent chance.

Life Event	Mean Value	Your Score
_____ Death of Spouse	100	_____
_____ Divorce	73	_____
_____		
_____ Marital Separation	65	_____
_____ Jail Term	63	_____
_____		
_____ Death of Close Family Member	63	_____
_____ Personal Injury or Illness	53	_____
_____		
_____ Marriage	50	_____
_____ Fired at Work	47	_____

ENERGY FOLLOWS INTENTIONS.

Life Event	Mean Value	Your Score
_____ Marital Reconciliation	45	_____
_____ Retirement	45	_____
_____ Change in Health of Family Member	44	_____
_____ Pregnancy	40	_____
_____ Sex Difficulties	39	_____
_____ Gain of New Family Member	39	_____
_____ Business Readjustment	39	_____
_____ Change in Financial State	38	_____
_____ Death of Close Friend	37	_____
_____ Change to Different Line of Work	36	_____
_____ Change in Number of Arguments with Spouse	35	_____
_____ Mortgage over $10,000	31	_____
_____ Foreclosure of Mortgage or Loan	30	_____
_____ Change in Responsibilities at Work	29	_____
_____ Son or Daughter Leaving Home	29	_____
_____ Trouble with In-laws	29	_____
_____ Outstanding Personal Achievement	28	_____
_____ Wife Begins or Stops Work	26	_____
_____ Begin or End School	26	_____
_____ Change in Living Conditions	25	_____
_____ Revision of Personal Habits	24	_____
_____ Trouble with Boss	23	_____
_____ Change in Work Hours or Conditions	20	_____
_____ Change in Residence	20	_____
_____ Change in Schools	20	_____
_____ Change in Recreation	19	_____

HAVE A HEART. USE YOUR OWN NUCLEAR ENERGY.

Life Event	Mean Value	Your Score
_____ Change in Church Activities	19	_____
_____ Change in Social Activities	18	_____
_____ Mortgage or Loan Less Than $10,000	17	_____
_____ Change in Sleeping Habits	16	_____
_____ Change in Number of Family Get-togethers	15	_____
_____ Change in Eating Habits	15	_____
_____ Vacation	13	_____
_____ Christmas	12	_____
_____ Minor Violations of the Law	11	_____
	Your Total	_____

This scale demonstrates something extremely interesting. We may be stressed by happy or unhappy events, by success or by failure. Even by vacations! Much fatigue is caused by too much of a good thing—food, drink, travel, entertainment, work. Our adrenal glands get exhausted from being held too long at full-speed-ahead.

But the Holmes-Rahe scale is deceptive because of what it neglects to mention. Stress and fatigue also result from doing too little. The unlived life is terribly tiring. The void sucks the life from us. Unfulfilled potentiality creates psychological toxins. Nothing tires me so consistently as not being me.

Much persistent fatigue is disguised boredom and shame. One fortyish, successful man told me: "I am tired a lot. Much of the time I drag around and have about half my 'real' energy. I eat well and sleep enough and generally take pretty good care of my body. I don't even overwork, although I often complain about how much I have to do and how hard it is. If I am real honest with

"FIGHTING" STRESS IS LIKE KILLING FOR PEACE.

myself, which I seldom am, I have to admit that I'm bored. I can imagine a lot of interesting and exciting things I would like to do. But I stay in the same ruts. Maybe I don't have the courage to take risks, to change, to try new things. So my fatigue is an excuse. I think most fatigue is probably 'rancid courage'—it's risks not taken, enthusiasms not pursued, dreams not allowed."

We must look for sources of fatigue in different places in different types of people. To stick, for the moment, to our oversimple scheme:

When Runners and Fighters, Type A personalities, suffer from fatigue, it's because they are constantly overstimulated and over-loaded and hence they fall into exhaustion. Their overstimulation may come from (1) the quest for excitement, (2) workaholism, (3) excessive competition—polite warfare, (4) conflict with friends, loved ones, family, boss, (5) keeping busy. This brand of fatigue is a mild form of the combat fatigue suffered by soldiers who have been too long in a battle zone. For Type A personal-ities, life is a battle. Winning is the big thing. And it is exhausting to live on a battleground.

Hiders, Type B personalities, usually the shy introverts, may feel exhausted because they are underachievers. They watch rather than act. They tend more toward the fatigue that comes from boredom (which we will talk about in the next chapter) than the tiredness that comes from an excess of excitement. Their fatigue is fed by (1) passivity, (2) feeling victimized, (3) interior conflicts, (4) fear of actualizing themselves in the outside world, (5) psychic rust, the accumulated toxins of unlived years. It is wearisome to live in a fearful world where we dare not show our true colors.

TOO MUCH OF A GOOD THING MAY BE WORSE THAN A LITTLE OF A BAD THING.

Lingering fatigue is only the first step into the night country. If you recognize your fatigue style—the causes and uses of fatigue in your life—you can begin dealing with it consciously. If caught early, fatigue is reversible. By knowing the signs and taking appropriate action, we can stop the slide down the spiral into night country.

The Fatigue Awareness Inventory offers you some handles on the causes (and thereby eventually on the cures) of your fatigue.

FATIGUE AWARENESS INVENTORY

1. Are you more often tired and for longer periods than you were a year ago? Five years?

2. Do you experience more or less stress? What are the major factors that create stress for you? Perfectionistic demands and unrealizable "oughts" that you impose on yourself? The demands of your spouse? Children? Job? Environment? Illness? How can you minimize it?

3. At what hours of the day is your energy highest? Lowest? Chart your biorhythms (emotional-mental-physical ups and downs) for an average day, week, month, year.

4. What foods give you the most sustained energy? What foods contribute to fatigue and depression?

5. How much sleep do you need? What amount is too little? Too much? Do you often sleep to avoid facing difficult situations?

6. In what situations does boredom make you tired?

7. What kinds of activities snap you out of fatigue? What are your best ways of re-creation? What forms of re-creation do you need every day, weekly, yearly, every ten years?

FATIGUE IS: OVERDOING, UNDER-BEING.

8. What are your first signals of fatigue? Irritability? Desire for food or a cigarette—something oral? Yawning? Loss of focus and concentration? How do you know when serious fatigue sets in? (If you have never done so, it is useful to stay up for a night or two and watch what happens to your mind-body-spirit as pure fatigue takes over. You will discover that much you have been calling the blues, boredom, or depression is simple fatigue.)

9. Where do you feel fatigue? Be specific. What muscles get tired first? Do you slump or hold yourself rigid? In the neck, around the eyes? What happens to your breathing?

10. Imagine and describe your least-fatiguing day in the last year. Why was your energy high?

11. How often do you use fatigue as an excuse to get yourself out of doing something you don't want to do? Make love? Go to work? Face conflict? Make a decision?

12. What emotion is just under the surface of your fatigue? Disappointment? Anger? Resentment? Resignation? Satiation? Disgust? Contempt? Jealousy? Envy? Fear? Boredom? Enmity?

13. Is most of your fatigue caused by overload (too much happening)? Or boredom (too little happening)? Are you a Runner-Fighter or a Hider? Do you live more in a battleground or a depressed area?

BRAVE YOUR DREAMS. OR BE DIS/COURAGED.

CHAPTER 6

SIMPLE BOREDOM: MONOTONY

Sign on a muddy road in Tennessee:
Choose your rut carefully. You'll
be in it for ten miles.

Into each life a little boredom must fall. Gray days. Ebb tide. You know the kind I mean. You get up and do the same old things you've always done, and it all seems stale and pointless. You go through the motions, but without enthusiasm. The monotony grinds you down. The old familiar routines seem like a prison. There is no exit.

WITHOUT REPETITION THERE IS NO RHYTHM. WITHOUT A THEME THERE IS NO SONG. WITHOUT ORDER THERE IS NO FREEDOM.

It's easy on these days to believe that Thoreau was right when he said: "The mass of men live lives of quiet desperation." Or to feel the futility of Ecclesiastes, which spoke of life as vanity and a vexation to the spirit because there was nothing new under the sun: "That thing which has been, is that which shall be; and that which is done is that which shall be done." Ho hum.

Boredom is a very democratic disease—it strikes without regard to age, sex, race, I.Q., or class. Schoolchildren and retirees, rich and poor, housewives and jet-setters, executives and farmers—all suffer from it. Boredom is an equal-opportunity unemployer.

A SAMPLER OF BOREDOM

Boredom comes in a variety of colorless models.

In Druid Hills, a wealthy suburb of Louisville, Kentucky, it dresses in natural-shoulder suits and decorator fashions, is polite to a fault, and sits respectably on Sundays in Calvin Presbyterian Church.

Mr. and Mrs. Bowden, Gary and Jane, were college sweethearts and have never left the storybook of the American dream. They are clichés, yet they really exist. She is shy and industrious and still determined to escape the dirt and provinciality of the eastern Kentucky coal town in which she grew up and the brutal watchfulness of an alcoholic father. He is charming, could sell yesterday's newspapers, cares about success, and is always well dressed. They have been married for nineteen years and have two children. Gary is the manager of a large printing business and can now afford the best of everything. Jane keeps house immaculately,

CONFORMITY MAKES CLICHÉS OF US ALL.

obsessively scrubbing floors and toilets. She is always busy. Their marriage is an old and dull habit filled with bickering and silent resentment. Neither dares to leave. Gary won't talk about it. Like most men he expresses his disappointment by silence and withdrawal. He drinks heavily. A couple of Manhattans at lunch with customers and three or four more on the way home from work. If he gets home. Recently he has been missing dinner several nights a week and coming home near midnight—drunk. Every few months he swears off drinking for a week, just to show he is still in control.

Jane is frequently depressed and talks openly about the failure of their marriage. "I know," she tells me, "that our lives have become deadly, but I don't know what to do about it. There is nothing between us anymore except the children and the past. We never talk. We still have sex occasionally if he is not too drunk, but more and more that turns me off because it is the only way we touch each other. Recently I have had to fantasize that it was somebody else making love to me or I couldn't do it.

"I feel trapped. I want out. But where would I go and what would I do? And what about the children? I can't see anything ahead except more of the same. What I'm most afraid of is that the thing in me that has kept me going will die. My spark is going out. I want more out of life than this. This marriage, this house, and all the pretense and fighting is strangling my spirit."

In the Okanogan County Jail in eastern Washington, boredom is doing hard time and going a little "snakey." It is part of the punishment.

HEAVY TIME AND EMPTY SPACE WEIGH THE SAME.

Lenny is thirty-one and has been in jail more than once. When he left Los Angeles he was determined to leave trouble behind and live the good life in the country. In rural Washington he could fish and hunt and raise his family. He never cared much about money, and regular work grated on his nerves after a while. But Lenny was always generous and would spend days helping a neighbor build a cabin or look for lost cows. His habit of poaching deer so that all the old people could have meat for the winter kept him in trouble with the law (Robin Hood and the Sheriff of Nottingham). One evening he shot a hole through the game warden's door and ended up in the county jail. Here is what he had to say about coping with boredom in jail:

"When you're stuck and can't run away, one of the first things that comes up is anger. I was locked up in a cell block with seven guys and at least once a day the boredom would cause a fight. It would begin over a card game or any stupid thing that wouldn't bother you on the outside. Boredom affects people differently. It is hardest on the guys who have a family, because they have more to worry about.

"The first thing you do is get a routine, or else insanity will get you. Everybody on the cell block has to be on the same routine for things to go smooth. You get up, shower, and eat breakfast; then go back to bed till eleven; then go out and look at the soup, which you usually dump out and bitch and grumble; then you try to get your telephone calls through; then you listen to the radio or read a book.

"Everybody gets a little snakey—meaning they begin to see things and get a little weird. After a while the walls seem to start breathing. If you don't move enough, something happens to the

BOREDOM IS KILLING TIME, OR DOING TIME.

equilibrium of the body and the floor starts to sway like the deck of a ship. So you pace up and down the freeway. Or you do anything to pass the time. Once all of us spent all day looking for a fruit fly somebody said they saw. Can you imagine that—grown men!

"And everybody tells his life story. One Mexican dude we called 'Talking Tino,' because he was always telling stories. Listening to him was like reading a paperback novel. He was a lightweight mugger—women and drunks—and had the scars to prove it. But he was honest; you could tell because he always told his stories the same way.

"One of the things that bummed me most was hearing some guy talk about his case—why he was in jail—over and over for months at a time. Same story again and again till I could sit there and tell him what he was going to say next.

"And then you fantasize. My favorite time of day—if you can have a favorite time of day in jail—was at night when it got quiet and everybody was lying there remembering the past and thinking about the future. You fantasize what you're going to do when you get out and all the good times you've had—sex and kids and friends. Then you remember the sad times. You kind of relive your life stationary.

"Everybody does time differently, but there are always days when it gets to you. You can tell from the vibrations when somebody is hurting. Somebody will say: 'Skipper's doing hard time today.' You don't show hurt in jail. When you're hurting, you're just short-tempered or quiet.

"Indians do time different than white men. They got more patience. They aren't so hyper and don't seem to have so much to

MAKE THE WORLD SAFE FOR INNOCENCE.

get out for. And they don't talk at all when they're doing hard time. I'd rather do time with Indians, because white men talk too much. Too much bullshit, not being true. It bugs me when some guy tells you what a terrific criminal he was, how much he's raped and pillaged and plundered. And what big connections he has. I mean—here we are sitting in Okanogan County Jail, and who does he think he's fooling? Big deal. The Indian is more honest.

"But no matter what you do, a certain amount of insanity breaks out. You try to build up routines and defenses against boredom but it gets to you. In this jail there wasn't anything to do. No program. The boredom was part of the punishment. But if you don't fight it, it will center you on a nervous breakdown."

In St. Petersburg, Florida, boredom is being retired from life with nothing to do but play shuffleboard.

Jerry Nodman and his wife, Sarah, moved from New York City to escape the harsh winters. In the living room of their small apartment they fixed me a cup of tea and talked.

"I always looked forward to retiring," Jerry said. "I thought I would have lots of things to do. When we came down here I planned to fish and take up golfing and maybe grow a garden. But here I am, only sixty-seven, and I'm so restless and bored I don't know what to do. I guess I'm just too accustomed to working. I miss it. I feel worthless down here with nothing to do. Nobody needs me.

"So every day I make things to do. I spend an hour or so reading the paper. Then I walk and sit on the bench in the park and soak up some sun and talk to the other 'old people.' Yes, I'm

SCHOOL TEACHES US TO TAKE THINGS SITTING DOWN.

beginning to think of myself as old, but I really think I'm just unemployed."

Sarah speaks up: "I don't think it's so hard on me. I never went out to work, so when the kids left home I got used to deciding every day what I wanted to do. I can get a lot of satisfaction out of doing volunteer work. The hardest part is having Jerry around the house all day. I like to be by myself for part of every day. We're thinking about moving back to the city [New York] or maybe to a small town where we could be more involved in things. There must be someplace where they need old people."

In Tamalpais High School in Mill Valley, California, boredom is cool and affluent and old before its time.

Jennifer is beautiful, if you don't notice the tension around her eyes and the slight bruised gray-green pallor of her skin. She is, as they say, seventeen going on fifty. She is one of the most popular girls in the senior class and comes from a broken home. When she talks about the pain and confusion of her life she is very poised and laughs too much. Over coffee at Davood's, she tells me: "You name it, I've done it. And so have most of the other kids at school. I've been on my own pretty much since my folks split up when I was fourteen and I went to live with some friends. So, like everybody else, I've done a lot of drugs and far-out things. And sex. I lost my virginity when I was thirteen, and I don't remember how many guys I've slept with. I've got a steady boyfriend now. The other is too much hassle. I don't think we'll get married or anything, but it's comfortable hanging out with him.

"School? It's boring. Really. I don't know why. The teachers try, most of them, but there doesn't seem to be any relationship

MASS PRODUCTION PRODUCES A MASS.

between what we're supposed to be learning and our lives. Whatever that means. I don't know what I'm going to do. I mean, society pretty much sucks. I don't believe in the government and I think business rips people off. Adults are pretty fucked up, if you ask me. I don't trust them. I can't really think of anything I want to do for a whole lifetime. I guess I'll travel and mess around after I graduate. Someday, maybe, I'll get a piece of land in the country and grow food and live with a bunch of people. Right now I'm just going through the system."

Perhaps schools are the training grounds for boredom. At seventeen, Chris Livesay reflects the disillusionment of many high school students. "I've been learning how to be bored from the first minute I set foot in the door of Edgemore Elementary School. Schools prepare us for nine-to-five jobs. They make our existences as restrictive as possible. They set false goals for us, absurd rewards. Think about everything you learned in school by the time you graduated from high school. It just doesn't take twelve years to learn that stuff!

"Schools want to show us it takes a long time to accomplish things. It prepares us for tedious and nonproductive lives. Without this boredom-tolerance training in schools, big business couldn't exist because no son of a bitch in his right mind wants to sit in a little cubicle buried in papers and drenched in fluorescent light all day long. It takes time to teach human beings to tolerate that kind of crap."

At the McFarland Creek farm when the snow is three feet deep in February, boredom is cabin fever.

Hide your private life from the public eye.

John Edwards sits in front of the fireplace and talks about it: "Out here in the country there aren't that many alternatives in the winter. There isn't anyplace to go, and there isn't too much we have to do. We do the chores and cut the wood for the day, but that's all done by ten o'clock. So we read a lot. But still, when you've been snowed in for a month or so you get so lazy you can't think of anything to do. You wish something would happen. Anything. You want to talk to somebody, but you're so sick and tired of the same old faces that everybody makes you mad.

"The worst thing about winter is that you're left alone with your thoughts and your mind goes round and round the same things until it is jaded. You're forced back on yourself. When I used to live in Alaska an old trapper told me: 'I don't get too lonesome. I can always talk to the trees. But when they start talking back I know it's time to head for town.' Up north we called winter boredom 'getting bushed.' When some trapper or miner got bushed and started making trouble, the Mounties would sometimes take him to town and get him a drink. They always said: 'What he needs is the feel of a velvet glove on the back of his neck.' This cured most cabin fever."

In Detroit, boredom is mass-produced and as predictable as the assembly line.

Steven Blandic has worked "on the line" for nine years. "Boring? Of course it's boring! Anybody who tells you different is full of shit. How can a man put two bolts in a Ford chassis every ninety seconds, eight hours a day, five days a week, fifty weeks a year, and not get bored? They're always doing some kind of study and

FORMULA FOR HAPPINESS: MIX ONE PART CONTROL WITH THREE PARTS OF ACCEPTANCE.

figuring some little ways to make the job interesting, switching us around on different jobs or lifting our perspectives so we identify with the whole car and take pride in Fords, and giving us better breaks and vacations, but, face it, there is no way to make this job exciting. I mean, I do the same fucking thing every day. How creative can that be?

"At first you daydream a lot on the job, but after a while you don't do that anymore. You just put in your time. And you live on the weekends. If you think about it too much, it gets you depressed. You begin to think: what am I doing wasting my life putting screws in a chassis? But it's a job. And a lot of guys, me included, don't have much choice. It's good money, and it's steady, and people are always going to want cars, so I guess it's pretty secure. I think about getting out and starting some business of my own, but I'll probably stay right here till I retire."

We could go on endlessly in our catalog of boredom: there is the "jet-set" boredom of "beautiful people" who live fast and skate on the thin fantasy of personas created and nurtured by the media. And there is the "Sunday neurosis" of workaholics who don't know what to do with "free" time and think God made holidays to punish people. And the boredom of children who "don't have anything to do." And the endless pallid afternoons of the sick who have nothing to look forward to except more pain. And the grinding discouragement of the poor and unemployed.

If we are to discover antidotes to boredom, we need to find the essence of the dis-ease.

NATURE CREEPS.

THE ELEMENTS OF SIMPLE BOREDOM

What elements are common to all varieties of simple boredom?

Monotony. Boredom is law and order gone wild; everything is regular, organized. There are no surprises. Routine is king. Up at eight. Brush and shave. One egg, coffee and toast, and catch the 8:35, lunch at twelve, etc. Second verse, same as the first; could be better, but it's going to be worse. Our slavery to clocks and efficient technology has made our lives and our trains run on time. But clocks can't tell what it's time for in *your* life.

Monotony is inevitable. Human beings can tolerate only a limited amount of chaos and novelty. Our need for order and the semblance of control brings on a repetition compulsion. We strive to create an environment with not too many surprises; it helps us feel secure. When we are most successful we create routines and cultivate habits that are so orderly they become monotonous. In monotony there is safety. And without security there can be no civilization. It may get boring to punch the time clock five days a week, but maybe it's preferable to the anxiety that would come from having to decide each day, each moment, what to do with one's life.

Holiday Inns understand that the average person would rather be safe than excited. They brag in their advertisements: there are no surprises at Holiday Inn—same dependable, familiar rooms.

Every society creates monotony, because the human animal prefers boredom to terror. This tendency is old and universal. Buddhist philosophy speaks of the wheel of life—round and round we go, caught in the same habits, patterns, routines. Freud made substantially the same point when he identified the repeti-

NEUROSIS IS A RERUN OF AN OLD STORY: EITHER BLACK OR WHITE, LOSE OR WIN, VICTIM OR VICTOR.

tion compulsion as a part of the basic instinctual drive of human beings.

The need for repetition and monotony seems to be natural. Mothers rock their babies in a hypnotic rhythm and croon rondo lullabies. In later life we lull ourselves back into that remembered ecstasy by mantras and chants and dances and strobe lights in which we repeat a word, a tone, a movement, or a pulse until the monotony captures us and sets us, strangely, free. The hypnotic sounds of rain, falling water, or drums create a rhythm that resonates in the brain, silences distracting thoughts and inner dialogues, and allows us to transcend our everyday state of consciousness.

In fact, monotony is built into the natural order. Saul Bellow captures it in *Humboldt's Gift:*

> The history of the universe would be very boring if one tried to think of it in the ordinary way of human experience. All that time without events! Gasses over and over again, and heat and particles of matter, the sun tides and winds, again this creeping development, bits added to bits, chemical accidents—whole ages in which almost nothing happens. . . . It is agony to think of the groping of the species—all this fumbling, swamp-creeping, munching, preying, and reproduction, the boring slowness with which tissues, organs, and members developed. . . . These are interesting only in review, in thought. No one could bear to experience this.

We may wonder why we continually choose monotony, yet indisputably we do. Listen to one of your most boring friends and

A GILDED CAGE TURNS A GOLDFINCH INTO A CANARY.

you will find that it's repetition that drives you crazy. It's a rare person who in conversation can make a point a single time and then be silent. Even worse, notice that you impose the same kind of monotony on yourself. Tune in to your inner dialogue and listen to what you say to yourself.

You've just had a fight with your boss and you're now rehashing it and rehearsing what you should have said and what you'll say the next time. Notice how many times you rehearse the same scene and make the same speeches. Our inner dialogue is frequently composed of old tape loops that we run again and again.

Neurosis is self-imposed monotony—"autonomous complexes" (Jung), "engrams" (Hubbard), "tape loops" (Lilly), infantile movies that get stuck in your brain, "conditioned responses." Personality, or character, is monotony.

The normal personality marshals sufficient defense mechanisms to exclude dangerous and unknown stimuli and just enough windows to let in an occasional wandering minstrel. Neurotic identity crises come when our defense mechanisms have been too successful and we're encapsulated in the fortress we have constructed with nothing to refresh us in our solitary confinement. So we play the old movies with their stale fears and their unrealistic hopes until we become bored enough to risk disarmament and engagement. (In psychotic disturbances, the defense mechanisms have failed and too much strangeness invades the citadel of the self. Life is too interesting, raw, and terrifying.)

Captivity. Boredom is a prison. The cage may be gilded with the trappings of affluence, or grim and poor as a cell block in the

Okanogan County Jail. Our chains may be forged by economic necessity or by our obsession to succeed or be well liked. When we are bored we feel cut off from freedom. We are condemned to a situation from which there seems to be no escape—a marriage, a job, a temperament, an illness.

Even, or especially, the opinions of neighbors and friends can form the walls that confine us. Fear of disapproval binds us fast to convention. And the status quo is always tedious after a while. There is nothing more wearing than having to please somebody else. A vicarious life is no life at all: you seem to be alive to yourself only when you see yourself reflected in someone else's eyes. So you are locked into the false world of appearances and locked out of the feelingful essence of your own experience.

Take the simplest kind of boredom. You're at a large dinner party given by a friend. Your host asks Senator X to say a few words. Senator X insists on recounting (bragging and campaigning) the major legislation he has been instrumental in bringing to the floor in the last session of Congress. You have heard the speech before (also read it in his newsletter "Notes from Washington"). As he drones on endlessly, your attention begins to wander.

First, you find yourself having fantasies of stuffing his mouth with mashed potatoes and gluing his lips shut. Then you think about playing in the azure waters of the Virgin Islands with your lover. But you're stuck. You can't really get up and tell Senator X he is a hypocrite and a bore. He is counting on your good manners and the pressure of social convention to keep you quiet. But you're frustrated and angry. You would rather be elsewhere, yet you're a captive of the situation. Freedom destroys monotony.

BOREDOM IS A MILD CASE OF SCHIZO/PHRENIA. A SPLIT DECISION.

* * *

Situational. Simple boredom is temporary and dependent on the situation. As soon as the speech is over you get up, leave the party, and go dancing. When the whistle signals the end of the eleven-o'clock shift, you're released from the tyranny of the assembly line and you walk out into your own life. In simple boredom, apathy has not reached the center of the personality. You still know what you want to do or where you want to be but, for the moment, you are prevented from fulfilling your desires.

Bilocation. Boredom splits us and leaves us in limbo. When we are in two places at once, we are really no place at all.

For thirty-five minutes you have been waiting for your date to show up. As usual, she is late. You're irritated. You would rather be at the gallery opening on Forty-fifth Street, but you are suspended in time—not able to enjoy the here and now or to be in the place your fantasy pictures.

Fritz Perls, the father of Gestalt therapy, says boredom is selective unawareness that results from a split in attention, "when deliberate attention is paid to something uninteresting and resolutely withheld from what would fire one's interest." You concentrate on the frustrating experience of being kept waiting rather than on the pleasure of seeing her when she arrives or on the passing parade of people.

Time warps. In this limbo both time and space are out of joint. The German word for boredom, *Langweile* ("long while"), underlines the distorted sense of time in all experiences of boredom. Time drags. It is empty and burdensome. When we are excited, time flows and goes by quickly and we don't notice it. In our most intense experiences, we lose track of time entirely. How long does a peak experience last: watching a tangerine sun sinking into a jade sea? An orgasm? When we are bored, time is a hydra; each minute must be killed, separately. And as Thoreau said: "We can kill time without injuring eternity."

Disengagement. Boring situations cut us off from the sense of our self as actor. They sap the will and feeling of potency. As Lenny said, "In prison it finally gets so you don't want to do anything—even pacing seems like too much trouble." Boredom reduces us to spectators. We want something to happen—almost anything that will bring a little excitement. But we do not feel responsible or powerful enough to change the situation.

In short, boredom is an early stage in the dis-ease of helplessness which, if untreated, can lead to a full-blown depression or even suicide. Waiting for Godot—God, the boss, the government, Prince Charming, the next purchase—to bring excitement and meaning into our lives brings inevitable frustration. A life stance of passivity is a sure way to chronic boredom. "I can't" creates no excitement. A wallflower at the dance of life: too timid to be.

Stimulus hunger. Boredom is initially felt as a lack of outside stimulus. Nothing is happening, so I am bored. If only I had a more exciting wife, or job, or could fly to Istanbul, then I wouldn't

---

TO A SAINT EVERY THING IS EROTIC.

be bored. The problem, dear Brutus, lies not in our selves but in our situation.

There are people who seem more interesting than others, or at least more available. Only a philatelist can love someone who holds forth for an hour on the 1936 airmail issue from the Dutch East Indies. And some places have more charm and excitement than others. It is this commonly agreed-on hierarchy of what's interesting that gives rise to jokes such as: First Prize is a week in Detroit. Second prize is two weeks in Detroit. But we have to be careful about "objective" judgments about boring things, places, and persons. Somebody even loves Marcus Hook. And, evidently, numbers of people find *The Dating Game* and *Hollywood Squares* fascinating week after week. We are each aroused by a very limited number of the possible delights this wondrous world holds. The pornography that excites Jack may bore Jill. And whips and bondage are just strokes for some folks. If we could imagine a person for all seasons, an absolutely democratic enjoyer, a saint of the unprejudiced perception, he or she would be fascinated by everything equally, would be no more bored in Secaucus than Paris, would be so aware of the nuances that every situation would hold something of interest. The average John and Jane look in any situation for the things they are already programmed to find interesting and stimulating. If these are missing, the situation is labeled "boring."

Stimulus hunger is so central that it is usually picked as the defining characteristic of boredom. *The Psychiatric Dictionary* defines boredom as "a feeling of unpleasantness due to a need for more activity, or a lack of meaningful stimuli, or an inability to become stimulated. The last form is generally considered pathological and may be expressed as a need to maintain the status quo

THE MIND IS MORE LIKE A PLAYGROUND THAN A COMPUTER.

and as a stubborn clinging to stimuli which are without interest or meaning to the subject. Pathological boredom usually represents a defense against libidinal or aggressive striving."

The early experiments in boredom were based on the assumption that "normal functioning of the brain depends on a continuing arousal reaction generated in the reticular formation, which in turn depends on constant sensory bombardment." In 1951, D. O. Hebb began to perform experiments at McGill University in which he isolated subjects in a small dimly lit cubicle for as long as they would voluntarily stay. The subjects of the experiment wore plastic eyeshades and cotton gloves which were designed to minimize sensory stimuli. He found that most subjects lost the ability to think clearly about anything for any length of time, became irritable, and began to feel that the experimenters were plotting against them. After long isolation, many began to hallucinate and hear voices. Hebb concluded from his experiments that prolonged exposure to a monotonous environment had deleterious effects and that "a changing sensory environment seems essential for human beings. Without it the brain ceases to function in an adequate way, and abnormalities of behavior develop. In fact, as Christopher Burney observed in his remarkable account of his stay in solitary confinement: 'Variety is not the spice of life; it is the very stuff of it.'" [1]

Experiments such as these with sensory deprivation reinforced the naive view that boredom is essentially a problem of a poverty of stimuli. This is, at best, a half-truth (and a dangerous one, as we shall discover later when we look at the prescriptions that have been offered for boredom). Even simple boredom is more complex than these experiments suggest. (A good rule to follow: be wary of the conclusions of experiments done on college

THE READY-MADE LIFE PINCHES.

students in controlled settings—they mostly tell us how college students act in controlled settings.) In fact, boredom is as likely to be caused by an *excess* of stimuli as a vacuum of sensory input.

Perhaps more than half of boredom in America is the result of stimulus satiation rather than stimulus hunger. The American psyche is overloaded with poor-quality mass-produced stimuli. We consume excitement faster than we can digest it. Overconsumption leads to poor digestion. The triumph of capitalism is to have simultaneously produced obesity and malnutrition. We stuff ourselves with trivia and suffer from spiritual malnutrition. If there is junk food, there is also junk value. To pursue the analogy: as a diet of junk food generally suppresses our taste for what is nourishing to the body, so junk values gradually destroy our taste for what is satisfying to the whole person. As Erich Fromm says, in the bored character "there is a lack of appetite for life, a lack of any deep interest in anything or anybody, a feeling of powerlessness and resignation; personal relations—including sexual ones—are thin and flat, and there is little joy or contentment."

The extremes. Baker Roshi, the former head priest of the San Francisco Zen Center, says: "Boredom takes place at two extremes: where everything is already arranged and filled up, and at the opposite extreme, where nothing is given and I must decide everything." The "ready-made" life bores us because there are so few decisions open to us. When parents, the state, the corporation, or the mores of a community force us into cookie molds, there is no adventure. We follow the course that has been laid out for us. But too much freedom is also a problem. Where there are no guidelines, norms, or routines we become weightless, like

YOU CAN'T BE MODERATE WITHOUT TOUCHING THE EXTREMES.

astronauts in zero gravity, and have nothing to push against. Many people who are divorced after a long marriage, or unemployed after a lifetime of working, experience the vacuum as boring. They can now do anything they want, but they don't know what to do.

To keep enthusiasm alive, we need just the right amount of freedom and challenge. Studies of boredom in schools show that it is the brighter-than-normal and the duller-than-normal pupils who suffer most from boredom. Students with a high I.Q. are understimulated by school. They learn what is presented without effort and find it no challenge. Students on the low end of the I.Q. scale are often challenged beyond their ability to respond. They are overwhelmed with challenges that make them feel impotent and inferior. In a competitive system where grades are the ever-present reminder of performance, the poor students are defined as failures. To protect themselves against loss of self-esteem, children will often say they are bored when they really mean they are anxious and discouraged. Similarly, many industries are now trying to match I.Q. and job requirements to minimize boredom. Some long-distance trucking firms will not hire drivers who score too high or too low on I.Q. tests, because both extremes have poor safety records. If you are too smart, your mind wanders too much on the long, lonely stretches of Route 66, and you are likely to run the neon pipeline through Flagstaff without bothering to stop for the lights. If you are too dumb, you won't think creatively about what to do when your brakes give out on the way down the Continental Divide.

FRUSTRATION IS A VITAL SIGN; THE SOUL IS STILL BEATING ITS WINGS AGAINST THE CAGE.

* * *

Frustration. In simple boredom, desire is still alive and fantasy flourishes. If you feel the split between your present monotony and the fantasy of something exciting you would like to be doing, and you are frustrated or even angry because of your bilocation, then your boredom is a mild and easily reversible case. You are only on the edge of the night country. It is only when desire, imagination, and feeling begin to be eclipsed that we descend the spiral to chronic boredom.

SIMPLE BOREDOM INVENTORY

1. How often do you find yourself in boring situations?
2. What are you tired of? What cities, people, foods, habits bore you?
3. How do you create monotony for yourself?
4. What imprisons, confines, binds you?
5. What are your personal classics in the theater of your mind?
6. Imagine that you are a missing person and a detective is looking for you. What habits would give you away (such as bowling every Thursday, buying Glenlivet Scotch, sending for tobacco to Sherman's)?
7. Which of your habits and routines are nourishing and which boring to you?

CHAPTER 7

CHRONIC BOREDOM

Simple boredom has a way of becoming chronic. A monotonous job or a bad marriage grinds you down, colors your soul gray, and gradually steals your liveliness away. If you don't get out of a deadening situation, boredom becomes a way of life, or at least a dreaded visitor who returns again and again. The malaise, once outside you, moves to the center of your psyche.

The line between simple and chronic boredom is hard to draw, because the chronically bored usually blame their lack of excitement on the situation or the people around them. Blame and projection are major defenses. Sometimes outside circumstances do hold us captive in deadly situations. Political tyranny, poverty, ill health, institutional life (the army, the corporation, prison, school), all have the power to force people into monotonous routines. But often we rationalize our sense of impotence and we excuse our fear of action by telling ourselves that something (or someone) else is the cause of our boredom.

No matter what the *cause* of boredom, you'll go furthest if you take responsibility for changing yourself and your circumstances, take an active rather than a passive stance.

Let's assume that you suffer a chronic case of the blahs and the problem is *not* with the world but with yourself. (A half-true assumption we will look at further in Chapter 15, "The Politics of Depression and Hope"). For reasons you probably don't understand, you're boring yourself. Why?

THE STRUCTURE OF BOREDOM

Chronic boredom is a state of self-imprisonment. Here is a picture:

EGO: I LOCKED MYSELF IN SOLITARY CONFINEMENT AND SWALLOWED THE KEY.

One person may imprison himself by constant anxiety, another by striving to obey a thousand impossible "shoulds," another by excessive shyness, another by driving ambition. Only our styles of self-imprisonment differ.

Philosophers and psychologists through the ages have asked: Why is it that men and women, having been born free, are everywhere in chains? Why, and how, do we create prisons for ourselves rather than live in freedom? Why do we prefer known hells to strange heavens? Why boredom rather than wonder and joy?

To regain our freedom, we must study the prison we have constructed for ourselves.

In chronic boredom the bars of the cage are forged by warfare. Two forces in the personality exist in a civil war, and the constant inner battle drains our energy, leaves us fatigued and, finally, bored. The battle is between:

I want something.	I don't know what. I will not clarify or act.
Desire	Paralysis
Need	Apathy
Stimulus hunger	Dissatisfaction with everything
Craving for excitement	Inability to be aroused
Emptiness	Passive expectation that the world—other people—will find out what I want and provide it for me.

Most psychologists agree with Otto Fenichel, a member of Freud's psychoanalytic circle, that chronic boredom is a state of

EGO VS. SELF: DEAD-LOCKED, IN-MATED.

"tonic binding," an unpleasant tension resulting from our inhibition of instinctual needs. In classical Freudian terminology, boredom is a product of the conflict between:

Libido	and	*Ego-Superego*
The instinctual, childish, infantile aspect of the personality		The "adult," or socialized aspect of the personality

In a classic paper, "On the Psychology of Boredom," Fenichel says:

Boredom may be schematically formulated as follows: "I am excited. If I allow this excitation to continue I shall have anxiety. Therefore I tell myself that I am not at all excited, that I don't want to do anything. Yet at the same time I feel I do want to do something; but as I have forgotten my original aim I don't know what I want to do. The external world must do something to relieve me of my tension without making me anxious. It must make me do something, and then I shall not be responsible for it. It must divert me, distract me, so that what I do will be sufficiently remote from my original aim. It must accomplish the impossible; it must afford me a relaxation of tension without instinctual action."[1]

To some degree, inner conflict is built into the human condition. We were all raised by parents whom we had to obey in order to survive. Our earliest lesson was: conform or die. (To a small child, disapproval = the threat of abandonment = death.) In the beginning, we obeyed because we wanted to survive.

I'M MY OWN WORST ENEMY. AREN'T YOU?

Therefore, we were all confined within the home-prison of our parents' values. We weren't born free. Think of your original condition as like the little man in the box. The values of your parents formed the box. Guilt and shame are the two bars of the cage. To get out you have to break the taboos.

In the biblical account, Adam and Eve are innocent and happy in the Garden of Eden as long as they do not question the orders of the Father—God. But once they want to know the difference between right and wrong for themselves (i.e., eat of the fruit of the tree of knowledge of good and evil), they are cast out of their garden-prison and must begin making a life for themselves. If we obey parents and society and never dare break out, we'll sooner or later become bored with our secondhand values. Our personalities will be conformist, infantile, overdomesticated. We will repress our own questions and our curiosity and sense of adventure. To remain in the security of our childish condition, we must sacrifice the adventure of the quest. The chronically bored are those who have never let go of the guilt and shame and who live within an infantile prison, governed by what Karen Horney called "the tyranny of the shoulds."

Let's trace the process by which boredom becomes chronic. How do we become imprisoned within a psyche, continually in a stalemated battle with ourselves?

"One of my earliest memories was of my mother catching me playing with my penis during my nap. I was supposed to be sleeping on the side porch, but I wasn't tired and had nothing to do. So I started playing with myself. It felt good. So good, in fact, that I didn't hear Mother come into the room. She looked at me

BOREDOM IS UNDECLARED WAR BETWEEN DESIRE AND FEAR.

with restrained disapproval in her eyes. 'Nice boys don't play with themselves,' she said. Evidently I wanted her love more than my pleasure, because I can't remember playing with myself again until after my first wet dream as a teenager. When I began to masturbate I always felt guilty. Once I was married and had regular sex, I never masturbated again. I just 'didn't want to' touch myself. Lately I've rediscovered the delight of caressing myself. I guess I finally decided it's more important to please myself than be a good boy. As a result, my sex life is richer and more exciting than it's ever been."

This account by a middle-aged man illustrates how we get cut off from our own desires and shut within the prison of boredom. In this case it was sexual desire that was repressed. It may be any desire. One man of fifty who was undergoing a radical change in life recently told me: "I wanted to be an artist, but I let my father talk me into going into business. This was the only way I could win his respect. So I've been a businessman for thirty years and I've hated every minute of it. It bores me practically to death. Right now I don't even know what I want to do, but I know what I *don't* want to do. Last month I sold my business, and for the first time in my life I feel free. I'm scared. But at least I'm alive."

There are seven steps in the process:

1. I want. I like. It feels good.
2. They (parents-society-authorities) demand. They expect. They say: "Here are the rules by which you must live if you want our love and approval. If you do not live up to our expectations, we will be ashamed of you and you should be ashamed of yourself. If you break the rules you are guilty and will be punished. Here are the 'oughts,' the ten commandments."

INVITE YOUR FORGOTTEN SELF TO LUNCH.

3. I need their love and protection to survive. Therefore, I must do what they require. I must obey.

4. It is too painful to feel the conflict between what I want to do and what I must do to be loved (to survive), so I will repress my own inconvenient desires, dreams, feelings.

5. I don't really want to play with myself.

6. I want something (the original desire is repressed), but I don't know what it is. I expect the world to guess what I want and provide it for me without my having to risk stating what I want or acting to achieve it.

7. The world fails. The world is boring.

In short, boredom is a state of self-imprisonment resulting from: holding on to guilt and shame, the eclipse of desire, the tonic binding that takes place when I remember only what I should and should not do and forget what I want.

Usually the steps in this process are not conscious. We don't consciously experience the conflict between our own needs and desires and those of our parents and decide to deaden ourselves in order to survive. In retrospect (in therapy or meditation), we can recover awareness of the process, but at the time, the narrowing of our world takes place automatically. We hardly notice that we are unable to tolerate or explore pleasures forbidden to (and by) our parents. The prison of shame and guilt is built invisibly. The desire for forbidden pleasures is repressed. We can scarcely remember "the Garden of Eden" of our innocent childhood desires, what we wanted before we were educated to want only what was convenient, right, and proper (or what the advertisers in a consumer society have convinced us to want).

STAY COOL AND YOU MAY GET FRIGID.

The symptoms of our capitulation to guilt and shame are usually a long time in emerging. Boredom may not finally surface into awareness until years after the surrender of our real desires. Then, one day, we notice that nothing excites us very much; we're filled with vague longings but no clear idea of what would have to happen for us to be satisfied with life. The inhibition, repression, shutdown in personality takes place gradually (like arteriosclerosis) over the years and is usually well advanced before it crawls into awareness as chronic boredom.

In order to reverse this process of hardening of the arteries of the psyche and allow the blood of life to course through our veins once again, we need to look carefully at the shutdown. What happens to the various systems in the personality when we surrender our own innate desires and live under the tyranny of oughts, values, rules not our own?

CHARACTERISTICS OF BOREDOM: CONSTRUCTING THE PRISON OF THE SELF

Numbing. A bored person numbs both himself and those around him. In a minor way, the bored suffer from the kind of desensitization that is characteristic of victims of the Holocaust or other brutalizing war experiences. Robert Lifton reports that the survivors of concentration camps and those who suffer from "combat fatigue" protect themselves from the memory of their pain by "psychic numbing" and a diminished capacity to feel.

The chronically bored are victims of a sustained interior civil war. They inject novocaine into almost every aspect of their personalities to cease feeling the pain of their conflict, their

IMAGINATION IS AN ESCAPE ARTIST NO PRISON CAN HOLD.

disappointed hopes and aborted dreams. Unlike the survivors of the unthinkable brutalities of modern war, the chronically bored still retain a small measure of unspecific hope—a flicker of desire, a vague expectation that something might happen that would return them to the land of the living—("somebody, please, blow on the embers"). In true apathy the world has been reduced to ashes, the phoenix has been killed. The specter of mass destruction and routine cruelty all but destroys the heart.

Chronic boredom has reached epidemic proportions in the last decade because modern society has become a battle zone. Competition has all but destroyed community. Cultural change is so rapid we cannot adapt fast enough to keep up. The cycle of inflation-depression makes economic survival questionable for all but the very rich. The energy crisis, the ecological crisis, the failure in confidence in our government—all add to the normal terror of everyday life in the twentieth century.

The threat of annihilation hangs over everything. We are all living under the gun. Our old myths, models, and dreams are rapidly dying, and we do not yet have any myth that inspires and awakens us to hopeful action. The outer and the inner crises—our crumbling political and psychological identities—are too confusing and painful. Is it any wonder that we numb ourselves and call upon boredom to mask the helplessness and disappointment we would otherwise feel?

John G. is one of the chronically bored. When I first went to interview him I had the impression that I was in the presence of an automaton or a zombie. Although his face was potentially handsome, it appeared to be molded of hardened clay. No flicker

MOUNT YOUR NIGHT MARE AND RIDE TO HELL AND BACK.

of emotion, no blush of embarrassment or enthusiasm warmed his flesh at any time during our conversation. He told me in a monotone how he had sought therapy after ten years of marriage because his wife was frigid. They had made love eight or ten times during their marriage. He seemed to have no idea that his own emotional impotence might be a factor in his sterile marriage.

"It's true," he said, "I don't get too excited about anything. I try to stay comfortable. Life is basically absurd and I just don't care too much what happens to me. I know that a lot of people are afraid of dying, but I'm not. Oh, I'm a little afraid of the suffering, but not the annihilation."

When I asked what he did with his spare time he showed me around the house and pointed out all the mechanical gadgets— TV, recorders, automatic door openers, hi-fi, motorcycles. "I like machines of all kinds. And sometimes I race motorcycles." When I probed about his motorcycle racing, he told me how a friend of his had been killed two years previously when they were riding together.

"I was riding in front of him and I got to the fork in the road and stopped to wait for him. When he didn't come in five minutes I turned around and went looking for him. When I got there the ambulance was already taking him to the hospital, but he was dead." No trace of emotion in his voice.

"Were you very broken up by his death?" I asked.

"A little, I guess. But like I told you, I don't let things get to me. When my mother died I cried for thirty minutes or so on the way home from the hospital, but that's all. You know, different people feel things in different ways and intensities. I'm just not a feeling type. What's wrong with that?"

IF YOU PLAY IT SAFE, YOU'LL BE SORRY.

Eclipse of fantasy and imagination. To defend ourselves against the pain of disappointments, past and future, we shut down memory and fantasy. When we are caught in a monotonous job, we can still daydream about escape to the South Seas. But once ennui has become a way of life, we no longer form mind pictures of what would satisfy us. It is too threatening to fantasize.

If the bored housewife allowed her fantasies to run free, she might well get in trouble! She might imagine how her life would be if she had a lover who talked to her, or if she took up the painting she put aside when she married. And then the first thing you know she might start to make demands for more opportunity for self-expression. Oh, trouble brewing! Maybe it's better to "be realistic" and not rock the boat.

According to Fenichel, the bored person inhibits fantasy because of an unconscious fear that the forbidden thought might lead to the forbidden deed. Fantasy might reveal our forbidden sexual or aggressive desires, or any of the "childish" dreams we put away to win the love of parents and peers. Shutting down fantasy prevents painful intrapsychic conflicts from becoming conscious.

Creativity curtailed. Since creativity involves a continuing dance between the conscious and unconscious minds, between rationality and fantasy, boredom destroys creativity. Hence bored people reinforce their boredom by seeking jobs that do not require them to be creative. They remain in safe but monotonous situations rather than open up corridors of their minds and feelings that might lead into a presumably dangerous unknown.

The rule has exceptions. Some artists and writers cannot find

FANTASY: IT'S A NICE PLACE TO VISIT, BUT I WOULDN'T WANT TO LIVE THERE.

any way to enrich their lives and relationships—and hence are bored and depressed—and yet are able to allow their imaginations sufficient free play to create the alternative worlds that appear in their paintings and novels. Guy de Maupassant wrote of himself:

> I am terribly bored. . . . I accept everything with indifference and I spend two-thirds of my time being profoundly bored. . . . There is not a man under the sun who is more bored than I. Nothing seems to me to be worth the trouble of an effort or a movement. I am bored without cease, without rest, and without hope, because I desire nothing, I expect nothing. . . . Everything is all the same to me in life, men, women, and events. This is my true profession of faith; and I might add something you will hardly believe, namely, that I am no more attached to myself than to others. Everything is divisible into farce, ennui, and wretchedness.

For de Maupassant, creation was the only release from boredom. "Everything bores me, and the only tolerable hours are those when I am writing."[2] It might be clearest to say that chronic boredom destroys the ability to use fantasy creatively to enrich one's personal existence. Bored engineers may still design brilliant weapons systems even when they cannot imagine what might be more exciting for them to do than design megadeath. How, for instance, it might feel to dig in the earth and plant fruit trees, or run a small fishing boat off the Florida Keys.

To keep threatening (and promising) fantasies from dropping in unannounced and disturbing our secure routines, we keep very

ALL PASSION IS COM-PASSION.

tight control over ourselves. Keep busy and distracted. Psychologists studying the rapid eye movements that are characteristic of
dream states have recently discovered that most people have a
natural rhythm—a REM cycle: fantasy and dreamlike consciousness occur roughly every ninety minutes, day and night. Nature
designs us to be refreshed and enlivened by fantasy every hour
and a half! The capacity and need for a little craziness, a
minipsychosis, a brief psychedelic adventure, are built into our
neural program! To shut down fantasy, we must keep very busy
and distracted enough to block all intrusions from the unconscious.

Feeling is blunted. The chronically bored do not feel anything
vividly. Neither joy nor grief, hope nor despair. Things happen to
them, but they don't register. Camus' *The Stranger* begins: "Mother
died yesterday, or was it today?" John G. never wept for his friend,
and only one half hour for his mother's death. Since feeling is
indivisible, the decision not to feel the pain of conflict and
disappointment carries with it a deadening of anger, laughter,
weeping, and joy. We can only choose *whether* we will feel and not
what we will feel.

The effects of the constriction of feelings are more widespread
than we usually recognize.

Feeling is:

the heart of aliveness

our vibrational attachment to the symphony of life

the root of individuality

IT TAKES NERVE TO FEEL.

the source of our sense of worthiness

the basis for our judgment of good and evil

our inner resonance of the outer world

our most intimate act of *valuing*

When someone you love reaches out to caress you and you suddenly feel a flash of joy, your deepest being says, "Yes, this is good, I like this, I value this." When someone you love dies and you are convulsed with grief, your tears say, "No! It hurts to lose this loved one. Someone I value has been taken from me." When we cut off our feelings (because of the pain of loss and the fear of conflict), we sever the nerve endings that connect us to the world. We divorce ourselves from life (which must be taken "for better, for worse, for richer, for poorer . . .").

Emotional castration renders us impotent as persons. Surrendering our feelings and taking refuge in the emotional fog of chronic boredom destroys our personhood. All of the large words existentialist philosophers and sociologists have used to characterize the psychological plague that seems to be settling over the industrialized nations—alienation, estrangement, anomie, depersonalization, disengagement, nihilism, the loss of meaning—are fancy ways of saying that we are in mortal danger of surrendering our feelingfulness.

Modern boredom is a symptom of our crisis in values. It hurts to feel our lostness, to feel the impending collapse of the technological dream of building "Alabaster cities, undimmed by human tears." The old gods, the certainties, the agreed-upon values are dead. And we are stunned, trying like the ancient

THE BOTTOM LINE (THE PROPHET SAYS) IS JUSTICE.

Romans to pacify ourselves with luxuries, to protect ourselves from the painful knowledge of the collapse and fall of the American Empire.

Boredom masks a melancholy claim to superiority. While depressed persons generally feel inferior to others, the chronically bored are blasé. They are above it all. Nothing is quite good enough for them. Nothing is exciting or interesting enough to arouse them from their lethargy. Nothing deserves their enthusiastic support. From their safe citadel they look down their noses at the world and say: "Is this all there is? Nothing is quite worthy of me."

This assumed "superiority" is rooted in the refusal to be vulnerable, to open up to caring and possible disappointment. The radical "cool" of the chronically bored comes from frozen emotions. They have adopted the attitude summed up in a graffiti I recently saw: "Stay cool. Don't get personally involved in your life."

Sensory compensation. Once the nerve of feeling has been deadened, the bored person seeks some stimulation that will give him or her a sense of being alive. Diversion, entertainment, sensory titillation are supposed to compensate for the surrendered sense of feelingfulness. Quite often, the inner emptiness leads to an exaggerated sense of hunger and addiction. Obsessive eating, drinking, smoking, consuming are the most common ways of trying to fill the inner void.

Many studies of boredom confuse simple monotony with chronic boredom. In situational (simple) boredom a monotonous

AXIOM: NO SENSATION CAN FILL AN EMOTIONAL VOID.

environment may well lack meaningful stimuli. A chronically bored person is quite capable of finding nothing exciting in the middle of Manhattan or Malibu.

Disinclination to action. The bored are spectators rather than actors. Once we cut off feelings, blunt desires, and repress the fantasies of what would truly satisfy us, the impulse to action is destroyed. We act because we *desire* something—a lover, a car, a house, a more just society—that we *imagine* we can get. The bored adopt a passive-dependent strategy for manipulating the world. Like the ideal Momma, others are supposed to guess what they want and provide it for them.

This passive stance is frequently at the heart of sexual and marital problems. One or both partners expect the other to anticipate their needs and fulfill them: "If you really loved me you would do what pleases me without my having to tell you what it is."

Even people who are seemingly the most active are often inwardly passive. The stimulus addict wants the food, the drug, the latest thrill to "turn him on." Isolated from their true feelings, addicts of all sorts lose the inner compass that might give them a sense of the right direction and the right action.

One young housewife explained to me: "I want to buy a couch. But I don't dare. I think my husband would hate what I pick out. I'm so afraid of making a mistake that I can't do anything. I'm paralyzed."

Pierre Janet, one of the early founders of psychology, said that

HELP! I'M A PRISONER IN A VACUUM. NOTHING HAS HAPPENED TO ME YET.

the fear of action was the essential element in the feeling of melancholia (an early name for boredom-depression):

> What happens when we are afraid of an object? A radical change takes place: the characteristic act is stopped, completely inhibited. If for some reason or other the fruit we want frightens us, seems to be spoiled, rotten, or poisoned, we don't want to eat it, we stop eating it and even wanting it, for wanting a fruit is the beginning of the act of eating it, and this act is then stopped even in its germ. If the mountain path that invited us to walk frightens us, we stop our promenade, we become disgusted with it. If a man to whom we want to speak, from whom we want to ask something, frightens us, we stop talking to him, and we have not the slightest desire to have anything to do with him.[3]

Chronic boredom is the result of a sin of omission. It is the sting of nonbeing, the pain of the unlived life, the roads not explored, the risks not taken, the persons not loved, the thoughts not thought, the feelings not savored. It is the dull ache of the possibilities we put to death, not because they were incompatible with those we choose to actualize, but because of our timidity and preoccupation. A tedious life is very near to the Christian notion of sin, which St. Paul said was the sting of living death.

Virile action involves some guilt. When we act we break some taboo, incur some displeasure, disappoint somebody. Therefore, a shadow of terror goes with action. When we do not risk and act, we incur real shame. We avoid anxiety and the shadow of terror,

---

ARE YOU TIED UP IN K/NOTS?

but we are cursed with boredom. An active life makes mistakes inevitable and therefore requires forgiveness. A passive life is molded by others. It is a victim's life. No hits, no runs, no errors. But it exacts a terrible price. It shuts us within the prison of ourselves and we remain alone with our resentment and the painful memories of our undared hopes. "Of all sad words of tongue or pen, these are the saddest: 'It might have been.'"

Sometimes I think there are only two polestars a person may choose to follow, two radical alternatives, north or south. Either we go toward decision, risk, action, individuation, guilt, self-definition, forgiveness, the joy of being a person, or toward indecision, security, conformity, shame, "innocence," boredom, superiority—either the engaged life or the spectator's life.

The loss of freedom. Once desire and action are repressed, freedom dies by inches. When we are imprisoned either by imposed monotony or by our own decision not to feel or act, the capacity for freedom atrophies. If nothing matters very much, then the choice between A and B and C is trivial. Freedom is bound up with risk, value, and effort.

Marjorie, a forty-two-year-old employee of the Department of Motor Vehicles, told me: "When I first came here I tried to change things. I was always in trouble with the boss. I felt full of piss and vinegar. Over the years I've learned to go along with the way things are done. But now I feel like a cog in a wheel. I'm afraid to stir up too much trouble because I need the job. Anyway, I just don't care that much anymore. I'll tell you something: there is only

WHAT CONVICT/IONS KEEP YOU IN SOLITARY CONFINEMENT?

one thing people have invented that will survive as well as a cockroach, and that's bureaucracy. It's bigger than all of us."

Here in a nutshell is the picture of how and why we choose boredom over freedom. It is a womb, safe and sanitary. You can't be hurt if you won't feel and you can't be disappointed if you won't care. Nothing can get to you if you repeat the litany:

It doesn't matter.

It's not worth getting excited about.

I'd rather not risk it.

Why fight the system?

Find out what they want and give it to them.

Why should I care?

I don't let anything bother me.

The chronically bored are unreachable. In the prison of the self no one really touches you. Any real contact with a flesh-and-blood person involves becoming vulnerable. If I love you I will feel your pain and your pleasure. And since that is too frightening, I must keep close watch on my boundaries and keep the border guards alert to any possible invasion of my territory. The door of the prison must be unlocked from the inside. Stephen Vincent Benét captures the loneliness in Lincoln's soliloquy in *John Brown's Body*:

BOREDOM IS RANCID ANGER.

That prison is ourselves that we have built
And, being so, its loneliness is just,
And, being so, its loneliness endures.
But, if another came,
    What would we say?
What can the blind say, given back their eyes?
No, it must be as it has always been.
We are all prisoners in that degree
And will remain so, but I think I know
This—God is not a jailer. . . .[4]

Resignation, resentment, and rage. Just half an inch beneath the blasé surface of boredom is a caldron of seething resentment and rage. As Lenny said about boredom in prison: "The first thing that comes up is anger." If another person or a situation holds us captive, it is healthy to react with alarm and anger: "How dare you waste my time? How dare you steal my energy and demand my attention for such trivial matters?"

Any dictatorship, Fascist government, or tyrannical political system that imposes uniformity and demands obedience of its citizens tries to enforce a reign of boredom by the use of terror. In such situations only those who kept a sense of outrage and rebellion alive within themselves escape the plague of mass conformity, anomie, and ennui that settles over every regimented society.

The chronically bored, however, are afraid of feeling and do not let their anger surface. Their dissatisfaction and disappointment fester, turn to in-rage and resentment. Since they will not take responsibility for their own decision "to bore themselves to death," they are threatened by anyone who shows enthusiasm and

---

FORMULA FOR VIOLENCE: CHRONIC BOREDOM + REPRESSION OF AWARENESS.

joie de vivre. Have you ever noticed how a depressed person can "bring you down," make you feel blue? The bored have deadened themselves and they want nothing alive around them to remind them of their failure. Secretly they want to turn everyone else into zombies so they will not feel so alone. Their yawns are designed to put you to sleep. Their studied lack of enthusiasm and criticism is an unconscious strategy to reduce everything excellent to mediocrity. Their monotone is a siren song to lure you into their monotonous world. Nietzsche pointed out that when our will to self-affirmation is surrendered we cease to admire and begin to resent anyone in our ambience who is naturally exuberant.

Rather than face the pain and rage we feel toward ourselves for our self-betrayal, we project our anger (but in an unconscious, "safe" way) outward in the penny-ante form of resentment. The "superiority" of the bored is cowardly anger—anger that never dares to emerge hot and direct but sneaks around and hides in the continual criticisms, judgments, and resentments they harbor for everything and everyone who is "beneath" them.

The bored and resentful are always looking for an occasion to stir up violence. Dostoyevski said in *Notes from the Underground*: "Boredom may lead you to anything. It is boredom that sets one sticking golden pins into people." Violence allows those who have deadened themselves to feel alive and to visit vengeance on those upon whom they have projected their resentment.

Since the bored lack the capacity for individual risk taking and action, they inevitably huddle together in a mass. They need a group to give them the courage to have an enemy, to do violence, to destroy, to make war. The gang, the mob, the party, the army, the nation, the corporation—only within these conglomerates can resentment burst into murderous rage under the anonymous

---

Turn your in-rage out.

cloak of conformity. A mob gives us permission to feel hate (whose real source is self-betrayal) and purge it on some scapegoat. Rather than admit the guilt of their own moral suicide, their resignation from life, the chronically bored seek to kill or do violence to others. The will to self-destruction is turned outward. Nowhere has this become more blatant than among the Spanish Fascists whose motto was "Long live death." Those who will not create prove their potency by destroying.

In a fascinating study, "Body Pleasure and the Origins of Violence."[5] James Prescott has shown that "deprivation of body pleasure throughout life—particularly during the formative periods of infancy, childhood, and adolescence—is very closely related to the amount of warfare and interpersonal violence" in a culture. Those cultures most repressive of sensuality and sexuality are the most violent. When pleasure is high, violence is low. And vice versa. Pleasure and violence, it seems, have a reciprocal relationship; the presence of one inhibits the other. If we stimulate the pleasure centers in the brain of a fighting bull, it immediately turns into Ferdinand.

When we add up the wasted life, the emptiness, the loneliness, and the violence that are direct spin-offs of boredom, it is clear that we are in urgent need of creative ways to deal with the demon of noontide. Otherwise we might, literally, bore ourselves to death.

In summary, think of chronic boredom as a prison without walls. The illusion of captivity is created by the ego, the persona, the shell of yourself, held together by shame and guilt and by the timid routines or compulsive busyness. Within the prison everything is dull and lifeless. You are captive in a vacuum in which a civil war is going on between vague forces and blunted feelings.

PLEASURE MAKES PEACE. PAIN MAKES WAR.

CHAPTER 8

THE DEEPENING DARKNESS:
DEPRESSION AND APATHY

Time now for a brief descent into hell and a look at some of the major league demons of the psyche that are close relatives of boredom. The population of the lower regions of night country is vast, and we will not attempt a modern equivalent of Dante's *Inferno* (although we are certainly in need of a modern demonology treating of the Spirit of Abstraction, the Profit Motive, the Lust for Power, the Swamp of Conformity, the Habit of Violence, the Arrogance of the Machine, etc.). Our aim is very modest, and sketchy. We need to look at some family resemblances and differences between boredom, depression, and apathy. Our concern is only to throw the experience of boredom in bas-relief by picturing it against the background of

MONSTERS ARE SHEEP IN WOLVES' CLOTHING.

more serious, "neurotic" (the modern equivalent of "demonic") conditions.

Boredom and depression are often practically indistinguishable. If boredom is the blues, then depression is the dark night of the soul. But once night has fallen in your psyche, everything becomes obscure and it's hard to tell whether you have the simple blues or are in the pits.

We ignore boredom and the common cold, the doldrums and the sniffles, because they seem an inevitable part of "the winter of our discontent." Life is often chilling and more often monotonous. Everyday existence includes much tedium. It's a grind, a rat race, a treadmill, a routine. So we take an aspirin and learn to live with it. We adjust to boredom as the normal condition and medicate ourselves with sufficient diversion, entertainment, and consumption, and hope it won't get too serious.

But ignorance is not bliss. And boredom ignored leads to depression. Type A, stress-seeking personalities tend to ignore the rhythms of fatigue and recreation and keep pushing to achieve their goals. They exert willpower and keep plugging away until they collapse into depression (old-fashioned nervous breakdown) or, worse, a heart attack.

Depression has become common and respectable in polite society. Boredom, on the other hand, is too nebulous to diagnose; we feel embarrassed to admit that we are victims of emotional poverty in the midst of our surfeit of riches. The man who has everything feels he has failed if he is bored. But depression! That is a real disease. It possibly even has chemical causes. And everyone these days is entitled to at least a minor identity crisis every decade and one major "midlife crisis."

DEPRESSION IS REPRESSION OF YOUR OWN "LOWER" CLASS.

Think of boredom as a vacuum and of depression as a thorn in the flesh. Chronic boredom deadens feelings and imagination so gradually that we scarcely notice the color and enthusiasm drain out of life. But something deep within—call it essence or soul or DNA or will to live—notices that life is passing us by. Something in us does not want to die. Something is hungry for experience. Something does not forget the promise of the rainbow. And this something conspires to make us come alive again, to feel. The shock that alerts us that we have prematurely retired from life is pain. When we fall into depression, nothingness is replaced by violent feeling and vivid imagination. The void is alive with demons.

Think of depression as a sudden and violent emergence of one half of our repertoire of feelings—the "negative" half. A friend who periodically goes into deep depressions recently told me: "When I am depressed I feel terrible. But I feel real. During the first stage of my depression I attack myself viciously. I feel guilty, worthless, and weak. I imagine all my past and future failures, you know, all the old horror movies play in my head. I remember my divorce and I anticipate how I will probably be abandoned by my present lover. I seem to concentrate on all the vile scenes that prove that I'm sick and disgusting. Often I imagine I have cancer or some equally awful disease. I go through a whole scenario where I'm dying in a hospital and nobody comes to see me.

"Once I realize I'm caught in a cycle of negative thinking and feeling—wallowing in self-pity and sucking up guilt and shame—I get even more furious with myself. Then I really get brutal with myself: I feel weak because I *am* weak, ashamed because I *am* guilty, and sadistic because I can't stop punishing myself.

"After a week or so of this kind of self-loathing, I go into the

PAIN IS NATURE'S WAY OF GETTING YOUR ATTENTION.

second stage—grief and mourning. I realize that I'm caught in myself and can't get out. I'm wasting my life eating away at myself. I feel I'm a victim and I can't help it. So I feel sorry for myself. I imagine all the things I would like to do but can't—like travel around the world, or climb Mount Whitney, or have a really good family, and mourn all my lost dreams."

Erich Fromm comments on this crucial distinction between boredom and depression:

> In some respects, the bored character resembles those in chronic, neurotic depressed states. There is a lack of appetite for life, a lack of any deep interest in anything or anybody, a feeling of powerlessness and resignation; personal relations— including erotic and sexual ones—are thin and flat and there is little joy or contentment. Yet, in contrast to the depressed, chronically bored persons do not tend to torture themselves by feelings of guilt or sin, they are not centered around their own unhappiness and suffering. They are extremely alienated.[1]

The crisis in value that begins in boredom is deepened in depression. When we are bored we may still believe that the arms race is evil or that racial discrimination and economic exploitation are wrong. We may feel vaguely sorry about the slaughter of the harp seals or the Brazilian Indians, but it is too much trouble to get involved. In boredom, our values are often intact. We know what is worthwhile, but we are frozen in a role of spectator. Our feelings are not strong enough, our will not potent enough to lead to action. In depression, the bottom drops out and nothing seems worthwhile. Life is meaningless, or evil. Caught in the tentacles of the negative imagination, the depressed person feels a victim of a dirty trick, a plaything of a malevolent universe.

Watch faces carefully and you will notice the difference between the bored and the depressed. The bored are blasé; their faces never show real emotions. Although they may smile, you get the impression that you are watching a mask, or a bad actor trying to imitate a feeling that is not actually felt. The bored are never really shaken by a belly laugh or racked by profound grief. If you sometimes get the feeling at a party that the whole thing is staged, or that most of the people are more ghosts than real, check carefully and you will probably find that you or they (or both) are bored. If everyone around you is bored and you are not, you will probably feel, like Dame Edith Sitwell, that you are "an electric eel in a pond of flat fish."

By contrast, the faces and voices of the depressed often betray struggle and violent feeling. Furrowed brows, clenched jaws, sad eyes, tight lips show the inner warfare. Watching the face of a depressed friend, I think often of the lines of Matthew Arnold: "Swept with confused alarms of struggle and flight / Where ignorant armies clash by night." The bored are bland and have faces that are not yet marked by life—no lines. Superficially their airbrushed faces may seem beautiful. If you look more deeply, you will see they are vacant.

Depression is more serious than boredom in that it is more painful. It is also more hopeful because pain produces motivation for change. The boredom trap is difficult to escape because it anesthetizes its captives. As long as the feelings and imagination remain alive, the nerve endings of the psyche are not damaged beyond repair. The excessive negative emotions of depressions often

PLEASURE PULLS. PAIN PUSHES.

alternate with equally excessive manic emotions. In the manic-depressive cycle, the mood may swing from suicidal despair to exuberant elation in a day, from victim to superman in a single bound. In the manic part of the cycle a person may feel near omnipotent.

"When I'm flying nothing can stop me," a forty-three-year-old manic-depressive social worker told me. "I can lick the world. I work sixteen hours a day and don't get tired. I'm confident I can do anything. I just bubble over with ideas and enthusiasm. I make grandiose plans about how I'm going to revolutionize the state welfare system. . . . Then I crash again, and in a few days I feel like there is nothing I can do."

Through exaggerated and unrealistic feelings of self-loathing and manic grandiosity, the psyche seeks to heal itself, to find its way to a feelingful engagement with the world.

To gauge the creeping hopelessness of chronic boredom, we need only look at the true state of apathy. The vague agitated longing of the bored and the active inner struggle of the depressed have ceased. Real apathy is as near as we may get to psychic shutdown. It often descends when people are put in traumatic situations such as concentration camps, extended combat, displacement by war or disaster, or extreme poverty where they are brutalized and subjected to the control of others. Soldiers initially show anxiety and fear in combat, but if they remain in the front lines for several weeks apathy takes over ("what's the use"). When the deprivation of food, love, comfort, care is real, and not imagined as it is by the neurotic, the response is helplessness and surrender.

The apathetic give up hope and action. Apathy is a defense against painful perception, and it helps to avoid the overwhelming feelings of the threat of annihilation. The apathetic slow

APATHY IS WHEN YOU DON'T CARE ENOUGH TO BE BORED.

down psychic and motor responses, show no affect, lose their sex drive, and go into neutral. This passive regression to an almost vegetative existence conserves energy and allows life to continue. Since the traumatic deprivations of war and imprisonment are real and not self-imposed, they do not produce in the apathetic person the guilt and self-reproach that characterize depressed persons. The apathetic are innocent victims who have retreated from caring because of overwhelming circumstances.

To summarize, the family relationships among boredom, depression, and apathy are:

Simple Boredom	*Chronic Boredom*	*Depression*	*Apathy*
Acceptance of monotonous situation. No intrapsychic conflict.	Consciousness of internal conflict is avoided.	Conflict is becoming consciousness.	Conflict is between person and outside agents of repression and brutalization.
Tendency toward sleeping or daydreaming during which imagination is active. Boredom vanishes when the situation changes.	Feeling and imagination are repressed to avoid awareness of painful conflict between id and ego, instinctual aims and the "ought" system.	Feeling and imagination are active, but in an exaggerated way. Often oscillating between feelings of impotence and omnipotence, self-loathing and manic grandiosity.	Feeling is blunted and replaced by passive waiting to avoid further disappointment and pain. Imagination is limited to food, rescue, and other necessities for survival.

A BREAKDOWN IS A CHANCE TO SEE WHAT'S UP.

No shame or guilt.	Feel slightly superior, blasé	Shame and guilt and the negative imagination are active.	Little guilt. Hate is directed outward toward the persons responsible for the traumatic deprivation.
Dislike of the situation.		Ambivalence about the self and about "loved" persons.	

All these states share a feeling of disengagement, alienation, slow passage of time, paralysis of will, reluctance to act and take risks, feelings of helplessness and passive waiting, repression of some or all feeling, loneliness, slowing down of psychic and motor responses, dulling of sex drive, loss of sense of meaning and value. In the gray void, it is hard to tell the demons apart. Boredom, depression, and apathy are bloodless brothers. But fortunately the antidotes to boredom (like broad-spectrum antibiotics) work equally well against any of the malevolent trinity.

Now, having looked into the abyss of our dis-ease, we come to the more cheerful task of exploring the healing nostrums and revitalizing tonics in our modern medicine kit.

PART
2

THE
WHOLE-SOME
LIFE

In theory, boredom is easy to cure. Follow the example of the heroes of passion and find something that excites you: uncover a secret passion for painting and follow Gauguin to the South Seas; go to Africa as a missionary like Schweitzer; find a consuming interest like Freud's; become fascinated with organic gardening. Any enthusiasm will do. Engage yourself in life and your ennui should disappear.

In fact, the cure is not so easy, because motivation has disappeared. Strong desire has vanished. There is nothing the disengaged person wants enough to risk moving off dead center. Like Willy Loman, the bored man has lost his dreams.

Fortunately there are many ways to recover passion and zest for

life. It is like peeling an orange: you can start anywhere. As we
have seen in our analysis, boredom affects every part of the personality—imagination, feeling, will, memory, perception, the
inclination toward our action. We can begin by revitalizing any of
these capacities. In the human body and personality, any increase
of health and vitality in any organ or faculty increases the
whole-someness of the entire organism. Boredom is a symptom
signaling that the whole person is not well tuned, not functioning
at full capacity.

In the San Diego Zoo, there is a cheetah who has a 100-foot
run in which it can scarcely trot. The sign on the cage says: "In
open country this animal can run sixty miles an hour." To "be
vital," we must give the personality room to stretch out and run,
to use its full potential.

The secret is: you can both dis-ease and heal yourself; the
prison is guarded by your own guilt and shame; the stalemate is
between different subpersonalities within yourself; the vacuum is
created by your a-void-dance of yourself. Boredom means you
haven't said hello to yourself and the world. You haven't yet
discovered the whole-some life.

Pick any of the following chapters that appeal to you most and
use it as a starting point. Explore any part of yourself and you will
be led toward the greater whole. The goddess Hygeia, the patron
of health, is very forgiving. She asks only that you keep opening
up to the life within you.

THE UPWARD SPIRAL:
A PREVIEW

Imagine that the road out of Night Country begins on the Plains of Silence.

Your journey starts when you cease running and allow yourself to do nothing.

In Emptiness you learn the Art of Simple Attention. Look. Listen. Touch. Taste. Smell.

The Habit of Awareness carries you through the Gateway of Guilt and Shame.

As you begin to leave your old personality behind, you enter the Fields of Fantasy and the Forest of Feeling. A thousand frivolous dreams flit across your imagination and die as quickly as

BOREDOM IS KEEPING A/PART FROM IT ALL. PASSION IS A WHOLESOME LIFE.

they were born. Strange emotions move through your body. For a while you are in the darkness of numbness, pain, disappointment, anger, grief. And then you come into a clearing where empathy, sympathy, and compassion dwell.

After you have learned to be at home in Feeling and Wish, you begin the struggle upward through your Tangled Wants and Conflicting Values until you reach Clarity of Desire.

Before you now looms the Chasm of Decision. You pause and deliberate. You strengthen your Will. You gather your Resolve.

With a mighty effort you leap into Action.

The Real World is filled with Wonder and Terror. You are frequently confused. Pleasure and Pain both visit you. Boredom and Depression evaporate as you enter into the Adventure of Life.

CHAPTER 9

THE JOYFUL ART
OF DOING NOTHING

The first thing to do about your boredom or the blues is nothing. Don't get a hobby! Don't turn on the TV! Don't find something interesting to do! Don't buy something! Don't take up volunteer work! Don't expand your business! Don't have an affair! Don 't take a trip! Don't change jobs! There is plenty of time for all these things later, *if* they turn out to be what you *really* want to do.

Doing nothing is simple, radical, and nearly impossible. It is hard for most of us to do things easily. We would rather strive and struggle to prove our worth than follow the wisdom that was once

---

"Can't" is impotent. "Won't" is willing not to. "Don't" is just waiting.

inscribed on every railroad crossing (before they obsoleted train travel because it was too slow): Stop. Look. Listen.

When doctors prescribe drugs that worsen the disease they are trying to cure, they create iatrogenic (physician-caused) disease. For instance, certain widely prescribed tranquilizers that were supposed to relieve depression were found to impair the heart's ability to respond to excitement, so they deepened depression. In psychology as well as physical medicine, prescriptions often make the problem worse. Many doctors, politicians, and economists have recently followed the "hair of the dog that bit you" philosophy of cure; they prescribe stimulants to an already exhausted system. The quantity school of quality—more is better—insists that if a lot of something made you sick, a lot more will make you well. More energy will cure our economic blues; more spending will cure inflation.

Popular magazines often take this approach. To cure boredom, *Science Digest* psychological adviser Dr. Roy Dreistadt suggests:

Begin with an action verb—visit, go, take, write; in other words, don't just sit there, DO SOMETHING.

1. Start a new hobby like painting, performing magic tricks, wood carving, or writing poetry.

2. Visit an exhibition, an auto or boat show, a museum, or a planetarium.

3. Go shopping and buy a new suit, tie, dress, or hat.

4. Watch an educational program on TV.

5. Take lessons in social dancing, fencing, or parachute jumping.

"WONDER" IS THE GRANDFATHER OF ALL VERBS. "BUY" AND "SELL" ARE STILL IN DIAPERS.

6. Go to a lecture, concert, opera, ballet, or play.

7. Take a bus ride around town, or a cruise in a boat, or a helicopter trip.

8. Go to a bowling alley, billiard and Ping-Pong parlor, or shooting gallery.

9. Write an interesting letter to your wife (husband, girlfriend, or boyfriend).

10. Pick up a chess book and learn the names of openings (like the Ruy López, the Alekhine Defense, and the poisoned pawn Sicilian).[1]

There could hardly be worse advice. Unless, of course, you are determined to spiral downward further into Night Country. If you want to taste depression and despair (an experience that is not without value), keep stimulating yourself, do something—anything—whenever you feel a lull. And, for God's sake, avoid sitting down unless your hands are busy knitting, your eyes watching TV, your mouth nibbling or talking.

The wisdom of the East—the philosophies and meditation practices developed in Buddhism, Taoism, and Hinduism—offers a perspective on boredom that Westerners are only now beginning to appreciate. (Perhaps there is poetic justice. The West exported its technological know-how, and the Orient—Japan in particular—is the world center for the manufacture of telecommunications equipment. We gave them Coke, transistors, and computers that heat up the world with noise and explode "information" and data. Now we must import their ancient spiritual technologies so we may learn the cool art of listening to the silence that surrounds all doing. But in the irony of history we

WE HAVE THE KNOW-HOW. WE NEED THE KNOW-WHY AND KNOW-WHEN.

may be importing the balm just in time to cure us of the dis-ease
we have exported to them. We are seeing the wisdom of
voluntary simplicity just when Third World countries are de-
manding the right to be industrialized. It may be our turn to be
the yogi and theirs to be the consumer.)

In Buddhist meditation, boredom is regarded as the gateway to
enlightenment. Here is the explanation offered by Chögyam
Trungpa, a Tibetan Buddhist who ran a teaching center in
Boulder, Colorado:

Boredom is important in meditation practice; it increases the
psychological sophistication of the practitioners. They begin to appreciate boredom and they develop their sophistication until the boredom begins to become cool boredom,
like a mountain river. It flows and flows and flows method-
ically and repetitiously, but it is very cooling, very refreshing. Mountains never get tired of being mountains and
waterfalls never get tired of being waterfalls. . . . I don't
want to sound especially romantic about the whole thing. I
am trying to paint a black picture, but I slipped a bit. It is a
good feeling to be bored, constantly sitting and sitting. First
gong, second gong, third gong, more gongs yet to come.
Sit, sit, sit, sit. If we are to save ourselves from spiritual
materialism . . . the introduction of boredom and repeti-
tiousness is extremely important. Without it we have no
hope. . . .

Boredom has many aspects: there is the sense that nothing
is happening, that something might happen, or even that
what we would like to happen might replace what is not

WHEN THERE'S NOTHING DOING, TRY BEING.

happening. Or, one might appreciate boredom as a delight. The practice of meditation could be described as relating with cool boredom, refreshing boredom, boredom like a mountain stream. It refreshes because we do not have to do anything or expect anything. But there must be some sense of discipline if we are to get beyond the frivolity of trying to replace boredom. That is why we work with the breath as our practice of meditation. Simply relating with the breath is very monotonous and unadventurous. . . . Nothing, absolutely nothing, happens.

As we realize that nothing is happening, strangely, we begin to realize that something dignified is happening. There is no room for frivolity, no room for speed. We just breathe and are there. There is something very satisfying and wholesome about it.[2]

I quote this rhapsody on boredom at length because it is so startling to the Western mind. Boredom, a friend in disguise? A delight? A source of refreshment? We view it only as an enemy to be fought, run from, and avoided. What secret do Buddhist and other practitioners of meditation know that Western psychologists have not yet discovered?

The prison each of us inhabits *is* called ego by Eastern thinkers, the character, persona, or personality (*persona* means "mask") by Western psychologists. Our lives become tedious when we cling to the same roles, stances, defense mechanisms, tape loops, inner dialogues, habits, routines. Gradually we put wonder to death by holding on to the secure and well-known repertoires we have developed. We close off the possibility of novelty and refreshment because the unknown and the strange is too threatening. Captivity in stale routines is safer than adventure in the wilderness.

To escape the prison of the ego you have created by your characteristic ways of acting (karma), begin with the simple act of sitting, watching passing thoughts, counting breaths, and witnessing. Study the way you close and you will learn how to open. See how you construct your personality, erect your defense mechanisms. Become a student of your being. Follow the advice of Socrates: know thyself. Or of Gustave Thibon, the French philosopher:

> You feel you are hedged in; you dream of escape; but beware of mirages. Do not run or fly away in order to get free: rather dig in the narrow place which has been given you; you will find God there and everything. God does not float on your horizon, he sleeps in your substance. Vanity runs, love digs. If you fly away from yourself, your prison will run with you and will close in because of the wind of your flight; if you go deep down into yourself it will disappear in paradise.[3]

The moment you make the decision to be silent and study yourself, you will immediately be in the presence of something very boring—your personality. Sit and observe your mind trips. Listen to your interior dialogues. Watch your routines. Notice how you repeat yourself, day after day, how you think, feel, do, imagine the same things over and over.

CLARITY BEGINS AT HOME.

How many times have you had the same fight with your mate? Given your children the same advice? Remembered the same traumatic event. Told the same old story about your life that explains (and justifies) how you are today? Notice how you adopt the same stance.

Neurosis, the Western equivalent of the Eastern ideas of ego and karma, is being stuck in one way of seeing, feeling, and acting. Karen Horney says there are three ways we can relate: with, away from, and against—cooperatively, independently, and combatively. Most of us adopt a neurotic style in which we limit our way of relating. We become habitually dependent (with), isolated (away from), or hostile (against). Day after day you bore yourself (and others) by using the same old one-tenth of your potential self. When you become one of your roles—doctor, lawyer, merchant, housewife—and define yourself by what you habitually do, you construct an identity that is certain to get tedious.

Seeing how you bore yourself is the first step in opening the door to your unexplored potentiality. Do nothing but watch how you habitually act and you will begin to allow more strange experiences into your solitary confinement. Your world will get bigger and more interesting.

But beware of getting addicted to excitement, even the excitement of self-discovery. There are two certain paths to boredom: avoidance of excitement and addiction to excitement. Eastern philosophers praise cool boredom and warn us against cultivating an appetite for excitement because a craving for intensity distorts experience as much as an addiction to any strong drug. There is an ancient Chinese curse: "May the gods

IN THE STILL, SMALL VOICE YOU CAN HEAR THE MUSIC OF THE SPHERES.

condemn you to be born in an interesting age." (A modern version might be: May you be forced to live in California, Manhattan, or Paris.) Life is not always exciting. If you insist that you always be "turned on" and full of the bubbly, you will have to manufacture a lot of false enthusiasm. Intensity freaks get hooked on their own adrenaline and lose the ability to tolerate and enjoy the natural ebb and flow of energy, emotion, and intensity. Bertrand Russell puts it well:

> A life too full of excitement is an exhausting life, in which continually stronger stimuli are needed to give the thrill that has come to be thought an essential part of pleasure. A certain power of enduring boredom is therefore essential to a happy life. . . . All great books contain boring portions, and all great lives have contained uninteresting stretches. . . . The lives of most great men have not been exciting except at a few great moments. Kant is said never to have been more than ten miles from Königsberg. . . . Darwin, after going round the world, spent the whole of the rest of his life in his own house. . . . For all these reasons a generation that cannot endure boredom will be a generation of little men.[4]

Zen Buddhism claims that the real miracle of the enlightened person is that she or he is able to savor the unspectacular events of everyday life. An argumentative priest once challenged the Zen master Bankei:

> "The founder of our sect," boasted the priest, "had such miraculous powers that he held a brush in his hand on

one bank of the river, his attendant held up a paper on the other bank, and the teacher wrote the holy name of Amida through the air. Can you do such a wonderful thing?"

Bankei replied lightly: "Perhaps your fox can perform that trick, but that is not the manner of Zen. My miracle is that when I feel hungry I eat, and when I feel thirsty I drink."[5]

The masters of meditation agree that the single most important tool needed to escape the ego—or, to use Freud's language, the repetition compulsion that forms our personality—is awareness, or mindfulness. Pay attention to what is happening. Learn to concentrate. Become a gentle observer, a fair witness, of your inner life and of the world around you. This simple, and yet difficult, prescription will lead you on a journey through the self in which your old limits will be stretched until you can live more fully in the wide world of wonder rather than in the claustrophobic prison of the ego.

Finally, by practicing the art of doing nothing you may recover that revolutionary silence that is the source of delicious solitude and creative action. As Hannah Arendt says in *The Human Condition* of the man who has discovered the blessing of contemplative thought (quoting Cato), "Never is he more active than when he does nothing, never is he less alone than when he is by himself."

Perhaps no textbook offers more gentle and relevant medicine for the troubled spirit than the ancient *Tao Te Ching*, which describes the Taoist way of life. To cure us of satiation and excess, it offers marvelous emptiness.

AN IM/PART/IAL WITNESS SEES THE WHOLE.

Thirty spokes share the wheel's hub;
It is the center hole that makes it useful.
Shape clay into a vessel;
It is the space within that makes it useful.
Cut doors and windows for a room;
It is the holes which make it useful.
Therefore profit comes from what is there;
Usefulness from what is not there.

And its portrait of the sage shows us an ideal of alertness without stress that could well be a model for a whole-some life.

The ancient masters were subtle, mysterious, profound, responsive.
The depth of their knowledge is unfathomable.
Because it is unfathomable,
All we can do is describe their appearance.
Watchful, like men crossing a winter stream.
Alert, like men aware of danger.
Courteous, like visiting guests.
Yielding, like ice about to melt.
Simple, like uncarved blocks of wood.
Hollow, like caves.
Opaque, like muddy pools.

Who can wait quietly while the mud settles?
Who can remain still until the moment of action?
Observers of the Tao do not seek fulfillment.
Not seeking fulfillment, they are not swayed by desire for change.

SPECTATORS ONLY SEE THE SHOW.

CHAPTER 10

BREAKOUT: BEYOND GUILT AND SHAME

Observe how much you are motivated by shame and guilt and an unexpected path to freedom will open up before you.

As we have seen, the prison of chronic boredom is created by a stalemate in which our real desires and tyrannical oughts remain outside our awareness. Life in limbo—caught between unborn desires and dead oughts.

The first task of introspection is to examine how we have been programmed by the shoulds and should nots of others. Conscience *has* made cowards of us all. It takes most of a lifetime to stop acting to win approval of others. The eyes of Dad, Mother, God, and the Law (all, now, blended into the eye of conscience with which we watch ourselves—oh, painful self-consciousness)

THE KEY OF FREEDOM: STUDY THE LOCK.

judge, reward, and punish us until we, finally, learn to look at swans and blackbirds, good and evil, through our own eyes. Maturity is a gradual process of moving toward a reconciliation between "I want" and "I should."

When inertia captures you, you may be certain you are being held fast by some ancient guilt or shame. Stewart Brand, the creator of *The Whole Earth Catalogue*, says: "I use boredom as a sorting principle. If something bores me I toss it out. More and more, I trust my boredom more than my shoulds. (Within reason, of course. There are some things you have to do.) But boredom is a sign that says to me: 'No! Stop! No matter what you think you should be doing, you aren't enjoying this.' It is an important signal for me to change either my attitude or my behavior."

What are these mysterious forces of shame and guilt that control so much of our lives and yet remain largely out of awareness?

No one is totally free from guilt. We all feel twinges when we overeat, cheat on expense accounts, or yell at the children. But many people allow excessive guilt to color *all* their actions and turn life into a grim effort to repay some imagined debt or live up to an impossible ideal.

When I began my study to discover how much guilt and shame the average American experiences, I found that most people either denied or were unaware of their feelings. Many women, and most men, who were obviously harried, chronically worried, obsessed with success and what the neighbors would think, showed mild anger when I asked if they often, seldom, or never felt guilty. One woman who apologized constantly because her house was a mess, because the children were noisy, because there wasn't milk for the

EACH OF US LIVES IN A HAUNTED HOUSE.

tea, because she wasn't being helpful enough, answered forcefully, "No, I don't feel guilty. I haven't done anything wrong!"

Guilt is mostly hidden beneath the surface of our awareness. Dr. James Purcell, a San Francisco family therapist, says: "Guilt is the hardest emotion to deal with because it's so pervasive that it's almost invisible. It's like smog. Most people defend against any awareness that they are motivated by guilt. It's not okay to feel guilty. Consequently we feel guilty about feeling guilty, we get embarrassed about our embarrassment, we're ashamed of our feelings of shame. If you want to find out how much guilt or shame a person has you have to do some detective work. Look for the indirect expressions: chronic boredom or anger, depression, failure, obsession, timidity, impotence, frigidity, alcoholism, or psychosomatic illness."

Where do guilt and shame originate? Are they neurotic or healthy? How can we best cope with them?

Guilt and shame are like two mirrors every child is given at birth. They reflect the image of the self. Dr. Gerhard Piers, author of *Shame and Guilt*, gives us a clear definition of the feelings. Guilt is the tension or anxiety we feel when we have broken some rule, taboo, or law. When we do what the authorities—parents, church, state—have taught us we must never do, our consciences hurt and we fear we will be caught and punished. Guilt is always accompanied by a vague, irrational fear that we may be terribly injured or even killed because we have disobeyed. We feel shame for our failure to live up to an idea or reach a goal.

Shame brings a sense of anxiety and inferiority: "I have failed. I have disappointed my parents and others who believed in me. I am not worthy of love or respect, and I am afraid I will be abandoned."

GUILT AND SHAME ARE A PAIR OF UNHOLY GHOSTS.

It is easy to understand the difference between guilt and shame if we look at their origins. Imagine a child, any child, living in an apartment in New York or a farm in Wyoming. Every child enters a world that is already populated by giants—MOTHERS, FATHERS, ADULTS. The giants seem godlike because they know what we want before we ask and they have unlimited power to please or punish us. They seem to be able to read our minds. If we please them, we are rewarded by their smiles and their approval. If we don't, we are ignored or punished and we fear we may be abandoned.

Very early in life we learn that the giants have rules we are expected to follow, a list of ten commandments, a whole system of rights and wrongs, oughts and ought nots. At the breast we learn the first rules: don't bite the teat that feeds you! Smile! Not long afterward we are expected to use the potty and not to talk when our mouths are full. By the time we can toddle we are warned to avoid strangers with candy and busy streets. We are taught that we must believe in God and capitalism, that we should eat our vegetables and not talk back to our parents. As little people, our survival depends on pleasing and winning the approval of the giants. (Personality is the mask you put on in the presence of the giants.)

As long as a child cannot wander out of sight, the watching parents make certain the rules are followed. Threats and punishment are immediate. "If you pull your sister's hair one more time I'm going to spank you." When we escape the care and tyranny of Mother's and Father's eyes, nature, God, or society equips us with a portable parent—a conscience—to watch over us and keep us on the straight and narrow when parents or priests are asleep or out of sight. Conscience makes us feel anxious every time we so much as think about breaking one of the commandments. It is as

---

INTIMACY IS SHOW AND TELL. WHAT'S UNDER YOUR MASK?

if the parents had become all-seeing and could punish any wrongdoing from a distance.

Shame develops because adults always have ideals and goals they expect their children to fulfill. John, Sr., wants John, Jr., to grow up to be a real man. From the first moment, he lets Junior know by approving smiles when he is living up to the ideal. When he hits his thumb with a rock and starts to cry, Father says to him: "You ought to be ashamed of yourself. Do you think John Wayne would cry if he hit his thumb? Men don't cry!"

Gradually Junior is taught by example and preachment that men are expected to work hard, carry a big stick, and stay in control of things (including women). By the time he grows to manhood his head is filled with official oaths and confessions of faith he is expected to believe and practice. He must be a good scout: trustworthy, loyal, helpful, friendly, courteous, kind, obedient, cheerful, thrifty, brave, clean, and reverent.

Mother wants her daughter Mary to become a lady. She dresses her in skirts, warns her to keep her legs crossed and not to get dirty or climb trees. By the time Mary is grown she has learned that women are supposed to be pretty and helpful but not too aggressive. Sugar and spice and keep everything nice; avoid conflict and get your way by charm and service.

There is no way for a child to grow into maturity without experiencing guilt and shame. No matter how wise or loving our parents, they could not have kept us innocent and spontaneous. Every child must explore, test limits, disobey in order to develop an independent personality. We grow into adults by discovering our own path between barriers set by guilt and ideals that are protected by shame.

EGO IS BUILT ON A CATCH-22. IF YOU DO YOU ARE GUILTY. IF YOU DON'T YOU'RE ASHAMED.

Let's look at a typical childhood situation that produces a conflict that must be resolved by a child's decision to become guilty or be ashamed. Mother finds her daughter Mary playing with herself. "Only bad girls do that," she says. Mary feels the disapproval and the implied threat in her voice. The next time she wants to enjoy touching her body, she begins to feel anxious. "What if Mother catches me?" Now she must decide between conflicting feelings and values and between guilt and shame. Her body tells her it is good; her mother tells her it is bad. Is Mary to trust her experience or obey her mother's taboo? If she decides not to play with herself, she does not risk being caught, disapproval, punishment; she is a "good" girl; she allows her actions to be governed by her mother's oughts.

Unfortunately, she becomes ashamed in her own eyes when she begins to repress her own wants and needs. She betrays her own sense of good to win affection. If Mary never rebels, if she is never a "bad" girl, if she never risks exploring her own feelings and asserting her values, she will develop into a childish woman. She may well lack the deep psychological permission to enjoy the pleasure of touching and being touched. And she will sooner or later become bored and depressed. If Mary takes the other path and decides the pleasure is worth the risk, she must live with the fear of being caught and punished. She experiments and learns to keep secrets from her mother and to experience herself as an independent human being. She may have a guilty conscience, but she honors her needs.

Mary, like all children, must choose how she will deal with the conflict between her parents' and her own sense of right and wrong. Some children become specialists in conformity and avoid

BOYS AND GIRLS ARE NAUGHTY OR NICE. MEN AND WOMEN ARE GOOD AND EVIL.

anything that is "bad." They are nice and obedient, but they grow up timid and ashamed because they have never dared explore life for themselves. Other children break the taboos, pay the price of guilt, and learn to forgive themselves for any real harm they have done to themselves or others.

Psychological health requires transforming our infantile fears of abandonment and punishment and our inappropriate shame and guilt into a mature set of values. When we violate our chosen values or fail to live up to ideals that we honor, we will feel an appropriate, mature sense of guilt or shame. A healthy adult must take responsibility for creating a conscience that will protect his or her sense of what is important and sacred.

To see how healthy guilt functions, we need only think about what happens when a person has too little or too much guilt. Our ought system—taboos, ideals, morals, laws—is very much like the immune system in the body. If the body says yes to every passing germ, if it doesn't distinguish between harmful and helpful bacteria, if it doesn't inhibit those forms of life that are destructive, we get sick. But the immune system can also work too well. The body can make a mistake and form antibodies that attack its own protein and destroy vital organs.

A person with too little or too much guilt or shame becomes psychologically warped. The girl who can't say no, who has no moral standards, becomes a captive of all of her impulses or of the desires of others. She does not develop an ability to create lasting relationships. Impulsive people may be delightfully childish or criminally irresponsible. Psychopaths have no oughts or guilt; they do exactly what they feel like doing. Lieutenant Calley and the women who were accomplices in the Manson killings had no remorse. The worst

YES AND NO: WILL-POWER AND WON'T-POWER.

crimes are committed by people who do not feel the sting of conscience.

A less dramatic type of person—the gray blob—exists without shame, with no ideals, with nothing important enough to invest with meaning. Gray blobs generally conform, sink into the woodwork, leave no trace of a rainbow to mark their passing.

Obsessive moralists who live under what Karen Horney calls "the tyranny of the shoulds" are the opposites of the gray blobs. They are so concerned with perfection, with what ought to be, that they kill all spontaneity and pleasure. Their motto seems to be: if it feels good it is probably wrong. A compulsive moralist can manage to feel guilty for the slightest display of anger or for any "weakness."

One young woman with perfectionistic tendencies told me: "I should love everybody. I should never get bitchy. I should be perfect. I should be more flexible. I should have fewer shoulds." The obsessive person forgets we need relaxation and pleasure to remain healthy. An excess of oughts brings stress and illness.

To become mature, each of us must go through a process of examining the oughts that were given us by the giants. We must discard those rules and ideals that are destructive of our well-being and tailor-make a set of values that fits our own experience of life. The mature person creates and abides by his own ten or twenty-two commandments. We may choose to reaffirm many of our parents' values, but everything changes when we choose our taboos and ideals rather than having them imposed on us by authorities.

A vital adult will feel shame when he or she has failed to live up to a chosen ideal and will feel guilty when a freely chosen value has been violated. If I commit myself to marriage and value fidelity, I will feel a healthy sense of guilt if I have an affair. If I believe parents should take time to enjoy their children, I will feel ashamed when I am always too busy for horseplay. If I feel my

PERFECTIONISM IS A FAULT.

body is sacred, I will feel guilty when I smoke a pack of cigarettes a day. If I believe I have the potential to write a great book, I will feel ashamed if I never try it.

The mature conscience is a guardian of what we have decided to revere. It keeps us alert to our highest visions of what is good and beautiful and true. It is one inner compass that guides us on the path we have chosen.

But this is getting ahead of our story. For the moment we are interested not in overcoming guilt and shame but only in observing it. For now it is enough to allow yourself to become conscious of the degree to which you are guilt-ridden. This is not easy, because the iceberg of guilt is mostly submerged. To get a rough estimate of the hidden part of the iceberg, take stock of everything you do (or don't do) that keeps you feeling bad, impotent, angry, sick, bored.

Are you always saying yes when you mean no (and vice versa)?

Are you always saying you're sorry even when you have tried your best?

Do you try to please everybody except yourself?

Are you afraid to succeed?

Do you worry when things are too good to be true?

Do you secretly feel you don't deserve too much pleasure?

Do you punish yourself by overwork or worry?

Do you often compare yourself to others and feel inferior?

Are you too timid to try something you really want to do?

Stay calm and objective as you watch the way infantile guilt and shame push you around. Be an honest witness of your captivity and you will begin to notice your unborn desires pushing up through the humus of your dead oughts. A whole new self is coming to birth.

AN APOLOGETIC PERSON IS A SORRY LOVER.

CHAPTER 11

THE RENEWAL OF
IMAGINATION AND DESIRE

A lively imagination is a certain antidote for boredom. Dip into the well of your fantasies and you will find the elixir that will renew your sagging passions.

When you are caught in a tedious situation you can always turn on your inner TV and watch an adventure unfold before your inner eye. On my own channel 1 this morning, Sophia Loren and I are shipwrecked on an island in the South Pacific. On channel 2, the president and I are just about to make a decision about alternative-energy policies. On channel 3, I am enjoying the peace and solitude of my hideaway in a remote part of Washington State. When you don't want to Be-Here-Now you can always Be-There-Then.

BOREDOM IS CONSTIPATION OF THE IMAGINATION.

Introverts who have developed the power of imagination are more often alone than extroverts who depend on the company of others, but they are less often bored. Eleanor Robbins, a psychologist practicing in Berkeley, says: "Extroverts gain their excitement from the environment around them, so when it isn't 'exciting' they don't know what to do. Introverts aren't so dependent on what is outside. They carry around their own riches in their fantasies and imagination. If you're caught in a line at the bank, you can always eavesdrop on other people's conversations and try to imagine what their lives are like."

The early experiments in sensory deprivation showed that when people are forced to remain in monotonous environments they naturally take refuge in fantasy. Dr. Hebb's experiments, mentioned earlier, in which subjects were confined to beds in small, dark, silent rooms, showed that after long confinement most people began to "hallucinate" and see anything from simple geometric patterns to elaborate scenes of marching squirrels. Hebb's conclusions are framed in language that shows his extroverted bias. He describes his subjects as "suffering" from hallucinations and showing childish emotional responses, and he concluded that the brain needed constant sensory bombardment for normal functioning.

In 1954, Dr. John Lilly began to experiment with a water-filled isolation tank in which he floated. He reported that when deprived of outside stimulation, the mind became free of the limitations of the body and experienced altered states of consciousness. At times, he says, "I went through an experience in which another person I knew apparently joined me in the dark, silent environment of the tank. I could actually see, feel, and hear

ONE PERSON'S HALLUCINATIONS ARE ANOTHER'S VISIONS.

her. At other times, I apparently tuned in on networks of communication from other civilizations in other galaxies. I experienced parking my body and traveling to different places."[1]

Instead of judging such experiences "hallucinations" from which he was "suffering," Dr. Lilly merely reported the experience of what happens when the mind is relieved of the necessity of dealing with sensory input from an outside environment. Imagination is freed to travel into a thousand strange countries.

How "real" are these alternative worlds? That is a question no scientist can fully answer. Nor need we try here. For our purposes, all we need note is that when imagination is allowed to roam, it can amuse and delight us endlessly. The most monotonous situation cannot hold anyone captive who has mastered the art of the uses of fantasy. The mind, it seems, is naturally psychedelic.

Why, then, are we ever bored if the remedy is as close as our own imagination? If we listened to our fantasies we would discover that each of us has a thousand forbidden lives. We are more wanton, cruel, frivolous, needy, lustful than it is comfortable to admit. We are outrageous and fearful, half angel and half beast. We are filled with contradictory desires and ambivalent feelings. And the paradoxes of our passions (to be lion and lamb, whore and virgin, warrior and saint, gypsy and homesteader) are inconvenient and shatter the fragile compromises we have made. Would anyone love us if we dared be all that we are? Dare we allow our imagination to wander and explore all those forbidden desires we have imprisoned, exiled, and bullied into silence? Do we dare to take the antidote for boredom and risk being fully alive?

The trick for freeing the imagination and reawakening sleeping

---

MIND IS A GYPSY, MATTER A HOMESTEADER.

desires is to begin by granting yourself permission to indulge in fantasy *without any obligation to act out anything you imagine.* For the moment, commit yourself to do nothing except be a spectator of your inner visions. Do not draw conclusions from your fantasies. Do not make decisions. Do not change. Make an agreement with yourself that your imagination is your sanctuary; here you are free to experiment with any idea without having to pay the consequences of action. Put aside morality, obligation, niceness; merely associate freely with your repressed dreams.

If you have long been out of contact with your imagination, you will need to be patient and clever to lure it back. Think of your imagination as a frightened and disappointed child who has been told no too many times. Invite it into your awareness as you would any shy person. Gradually you will win its trust and it will begin to tell you its secrets.

There are many ways to woo back into an erotic relationship an imagination that has long been neglected.

Begin with dreams. If you no longer "remember" your dreams, you need to become a dreamer again. (Women more often than men dream in color and remember elaborate dreams.) Alert your psyche before you go to sleep that you would like to remember your dream. Let this invitation to your unconscious be the last thing on your mind as you enter sleep. If you wake up with any image from the dream, lie quietly in the position in which you were dreaming and try to remember the rest of the dream. Record the dream.

YOU ARE MORE THAN YOUR WILDEST DREAM.

My favorite way to keep a dream journal is to speak the dream into a small tape recorder I keep beside the bed. This keeps me from having to jar my psyche awake by turning on the light and writing. Mull over the dream during the next day and savor it as if it were an omen from an oracle deep inside yourself. Become a connoisseur of your dreams. Notice what themes are repeated and how they change. Pay special attention to any image that is emotionally charged. If you see a black horse and awaken in terror, invite the image into your mind many times during the day and study the feeling that arises. If you awaken elated and remember you have been flying, keep the feeling of soaring throughout the day. Above all, play with your dreams. Enjoy them. There are no "official," correct interpretations of what they mean. Share your dreams with friends; weave the images into your conversations. You will find that dreams are often previews of coming attractions.

Try daydreams. Watch your energy cycles. When you begin to sag you will notice you feel either sleepy or hungry. Every ninety minutes, when you enter a REM period of energy ebb, yield to the slowing rhythm of your body rather than stimulating yourself with coffee or sugar or tobacco and take a fantasy break. Drop out, tune in, and turn on. Take a minitrip to the reality of your choice. The next time you are in a boring meeting and your mind begins to wander, let it go. What do you find yourself dreaming about when you aren't looking? Revive your old daydreams. Did you want to be a rancher, a mountain climber, a writer, when you were young? Rediscover the fantasies that gave

HOPE IS A DREAMER MARRIED TO ACTION.

you pleasure and see how many of the old desires are still alive and well.

Try to program guided fantasies. If you are dissatisfied living in Philadelphia and commuting to Camden to sell oysters, begin to make up some alternative lives for yourself. Try on a different environment. How would you like to live in Questa, New Mexico, and run a fish hatchery? Or in New Orleans and pilot a shrimp boat? Fantasy is the cheapest and safest way to explore options without having to face the consequences of action. With sufficient imagination you may be able to enjoy the fantasy of an orgy without having to relate to strangers who may or may not be HIV positive.

In the realm of imagination all possibilities are interesting, in reality we are limited by our tastes, our feelings, our past habits, and our future hopes. In a fit of anger it is sweet to imagine wringing the boss's neck when you are passed up for a promotion, but follow the fantasy through to the end and the momentary vengeance is not worth the years in Sing Sing.

Fantasy is magic, because it puts us back in touch with what is still childlike within us. It allows us to play with all possibilities, to be god for a day, to invent the best of all possible worlds. For a while we are free from the law of noncontradictions and can love mother-wife-daughter as if they were a single woman, or we can be both our own father and son.

Every fantasy contains a kernel of something we desire. When we are most alive we are never consistent. We want many things that are incompatible in real linear time:

YOU ARE DIVINE CLAY, AN IMAGINATION THAT PLAYS GOD IN AN EARTHLY BODY.

I want to be independent and succored, free to move with the wind of my impulse and secure as Gibraltar.

I wish I could be president and force the military-industrial complex to beat their swords into plowshares, and I wish I could sit under a Joshua tree in New Mexico and listen to the desert sounds.

Many of these desires are fleeting. Some are possible of realization, others are impossible. It makes no difference to the child within us. If we keep this psychedelic capacity alive, we remain in touch with the nerve endings of our primal passions out of which creativity grows.

There is, of course, more to creative life than fantasy. But the free imagination is the starting point for the free spirit. Liberation begins here. The image comes before the action, the play before the work, the dream before the plan. If we are to recover the full image of our feelings, we must create a sanctuary in the imagination in which nothing is prohibited. It is only when we are free to dream anything that we are free to do and refrain from doing those things that make life most satisfying.

Mature desire and responsible action must always be in communication with infantile desires and irresponsible fantasy. Order and rationality are steeped in a caldron of chaos. We will see shortly how these opposites are joined in the creative act.

A word of warning is in order. Imagination is a necessary but not sufficient condition for a vivid life. We can OD on playing with possibilities. Life is no game. An excess of fantasy no less than a deficiency can upset the delicate balance of creative life. Some artists and dreamers become so invested in their fantasies that they retreat from the actual world. Imagination must be tempered by feeling and action.

DREAMS ARE THE VOCABULARY OF DESIRE.

CHAPTER 12

FEELING ALIVE:
UNFREEZING E-MOTIONS

To unfreeze your feelings, allow the flow of e-motion until the numbness is replaced by the pain and pleasure of liveliness. No matter how vivid your imagination, how strong your sensations, how virile your actions, you will be empty if you refuse to feel.

Since the most common way of trying to cope with emptiness and loss of meaning is to drown them in a sea of sensation—eating, sex, entertainment—it is clear that there is much confusion about the differences between sensation and feeling.

Let's begin with a series of thought experiments:

A LIFE WITHOUT FEELING IS INSUFFERABLE.

1. Imagine something soft—it might be anything—a flower, a powder puff, a warm pickle—lightly brushing across your nipple. Notice the level and quality of the sensation.

2. Imagine your fingers touching your nipple. Notice that the sensation is now in dialogue with your feelings. Whether or how much you can enjoy the sensation will depend upon what attitudes and beliefs you have about touching yourself. If you come from a sexually repressed background, you will probably feel some guilt connected with the excitement. The guilt may enhance or deaden the excitement—black lace or a shroud.

3. You are in a prison cell. The hand that has crossed your breast belongs to your jailer, who has just said to you: "We have ways of making you talk!" Or it belongs to a man who has forced you into a car and has a knife at your throat and has just said: "What a pair of knockers you got, lady!" How do you feel now? If you have a normal fear and loathing of violence, the sensation of pleasure will be obliterated by the feeling of terror. Your deepest self is being violated.

4. Your lover and you are lying before an open fire on a heavy fur rug. Both tenderness and desire are flowing strongly. The whisper in your ear says, "I love you," as the hand reaches over to caress your breast. Notice the interplay of sensation and feeling. Your memories of past lovemaking, your anticipation of pleasure, your feelings of being loved and loving mix in and heighten the level of sensation.

This experiment tells us much about the difference between sensation and feeling. Sensation is the response of the machinery of the body to some stimulus. It is a matter of nerve endings,

SENSATION IS A ONE-NIGHT STAND. FEELING IS A LONG-TERM AFFAIR.

muscle, and skin. As long as we are merely sensing we make only the simplest of judgments—it's pleasurable or it's painful. Feeling involves the beginning of a more intricate process of *valuing* in which I consider how the stimulus affects *me as a whole person.* Sensation is limited to the present moment, but feeling involves both memories and intentions. So long as the anonymous something stimulating the nipple produced a simple sensation, all you had to do was decide whether you wanted to have it continue or cease. But when the hand caressed you, your past memories and future expectations were brought into play. All of your fears and hopes were added to the present sensation.

This should make clear why numbing feeling and increasing sensation is bound to impoverish our spirits. Errol Flynn, the movie star who lived the hedonist myth to the full, once remarked: "A man can be full of every pleasure and still want to die." An excess of stimulus may exile us in the present moment and not allow us to re-collect ourselves and evaluate. Until we pause to register how something feels, we have not digested our experience—we don't know what it means. As long as I am only sensing the world around me, I have not taken a position in the middle of my own experience as a unique person with a particular set of memories and hopes.

A comparison of feeling and fantasy may make this point clearer. In fantasy I may *wish* for any wild thing. When I allow my imagination full play, I put aside my body for the moment and take a mind trip. And, within the realm of the mind, it is interesting and even pleasurable to contemplate anything. Wishing, fantasy, imagination are disembodied flights into theoretical possibilities.

Nancy Friday reports in *The Secret Garden* that some women who

---

FEELINGS ARE THE SYNAPSES BETWEEN THE SELF AND THE WORLD.

are horrified by the reality of rape nevertheless enjoy the fantasy of being taken sexually by force as long as it is disembodied. They may *wish* to be swept away—i.e., have a fantasy—but the moment they consult their feelings about being raped they clearly do not *want* to be violated.

We all wish for many things we do not want. Once we tune in to our feelings—our sense of the continuity of our self—our wants and values become clear. We leave the spectator stance of imagination and come down to the real world of history, time, and embodiment. In fantasy we remain above it all.

Some people live only in theory; they remain in the "might," the "maybe," and the "could," in the beautiful world of "dreaming innocence" where anything can happen. In the never-never land of "I wish," we are free but not real. When we descend into our bodies and feelings, we face our actual wants and our limited options. We cease being gods who may speculate endlessly and become existing human beings.

I know, all this is easier said than done. We can't merely decide one day that we will pop our frigid selves into the microwave and unfreeze our feelings. The habit of repressing feeling is deep and difficult to reverse. It takes a lifetime to become a feelingful person—so there is no hurry, no reason to despair. Understanding something of the psycho-logic of the emotions will help.

Why do we decide to stop feeling? And how do we go about unfreezing our emotions?

At some point, usually early in childhood, the pain of existence got too much to bear. The pain may have come in many forms. Let's take an example. Nora is twenty-three, a mother, a divorcée. She married early to get away from a mother and an alcoholic father who continually gave her enemas—to clean her out—and

IN A SINGLE MEASURE WE AVOID OR SUFFER PAIN AND PLEASURE.

told her she was no good. Although she is exceptionally beautiful, she thinks of herself as plain and is always fasting or going on a purging diet to purify herself. Her relationships with men are not happy. Although she engages in sex with a variety of lovers, she does not enjoy herself. Her earliest memory is of her mother wincing and showing disgust when she was changing her diaper. Since her divorce, Nora has realized that she lives more in her head than in her feelings.

"I know I don't feel very much," she said, "but I'm afraid to open up. Whenever I start to feel, I remember all my pain and disappointment. I wanted to be held and loved so much, and I can still remember Mother's feeling of disgust every time she touched me. It's the same way I really feel about sex. I want to feel differently, but I don't know how."

Nora's story is in some degree each person's story. We were all disappointed, frustrated, and rejected in some degree—loved less than we wanted, afraid of being abandoned unless we were perfect, terrified of being punished for our inevitable failure. The myth of the Fall is universal. Each of us is Adam and Eve, in exile from the garden of happiness. Only the details and the severity of our unremembered pain differ. Some children were battered, in fact; others were merely subjected to the cruelty of a thousand impossible standards. Pain, disappointment, loss—these are themes in the first chapter of every story. (Also pleasure, satisfaction, love—we can only long for a paradise we had and lost. But that is another story.)

The automatic response to pain is recoil. A dog that has been beaten as a puppy approaches you wincing and still expecting to be abused. This is the logic of pain. Our psyche and body move

IN CHRONIC TENSION THE BODY AVOIDS PAIN, KNOWS BUT WILL NOT RE/MEMBER.

to minimize the memory of past pain and avoid future pain. We seal over the disappointment and deaden the nerve endings. We numb ourselves by creating body armor. Chronic tension stops e-motion and desensitizes the muscles. We stop expecting so we will not be disappointed. We stop being open and vulnerable.

To unfreeze e-motions and disarm our bodies, we must reverse the process. Kierkegaard once said that when a person hears the siren's song and is bewitched, the only way to break the spell is to play the music through backward. To recover our selves we need to undertake an archaeology of the feelings, dig down beneath the tranquilized facade until we reach the living quick.

Only an inch beneath the dead, numb layer of the personality we encounter the pain we have tried to avoid. Either we decide to face it or our adventure in feeling is ended.

Much of the illusion of modern life has to do with what might be called the Pollyanna Principle—the idea that we can avoid pain: "Accentuate the positive, eliminate the negative, and don't mess with Mr. In-Between."

Life is not a bowl of Librium. And a good part of the secret of happiness lies in learning to suffer with dignity. Loneliness, loss, disappointment, failure, dis-ease are inevitable. The price of trying to avoid the unavoidable is illusion, or neurosis. Even if you jog, eat health foods, grow, meditate, and go to confession regularly, you will sometimes fall sick. You can't escape occasional depression, even by memorizing this book. Your best-laid plans won't coerce the future. Nothing you can do will keep those you love most from dying. You can never be fully safe. The fears of abandonment and annihilation are in the DNA. They are the Siamese twin of the will to live. So, don't blame your parents too

LIFE IS NOT A BOWL OF CHERRIES.

much. It is natural to feel the shadow of terror at the edges of your days.

Face the negative: your father and mother didn't and never will love you as much as you wanted them to. The government won't take care of you either. Nobody is as interested in you as you. You won't make it to the top. And if you should, it won't be near as satisfying as you imagined it would be. The most unacceptable thing we can imagine has already happened to us: we are abandoned, we will suffer, and we will die.

Any psyche, or philosophy, that does not begin with these unpleasant facts is illusion. Any one that does has a shot at happiness—human and limited, but real. Camus says that we can write a manual of happiness only after we have faced the absurd. Suffering may be transcended; it cannot be ignored. Embrace the inevitable suffering and that part of your energy that has been invested in avoiding-denying-repressing the "negative" will be released and become available. Surprisingly, our inner agreement to feel our suffering is what releases us to experience joy.

Knowing about the slings and arrows of human fortune in the abstract will not help you. Unfortunately, we suffer as feelingful individual persons and not as abstract minds. To confront your pain you will have to remember in detail, recover your own personal history of infamy and betrayal, open up your past, and reexperience those painful memories you would like to forget. Psychotherapy may help in this process, but it is not as necessary as the willingness to begin feeling again. Fortunately, the juices of healing in the psyche run through every faculty of the personality—memory, imagination, feeling, thinking, intuition. Once your intention to allow the resurrection of yourself becomes clear you will find unknown allies coming to your aid.

EQUI/LIBRIUM: "A STATE OF STATIC BALANCE OF A BODY OR SYSTEM ACTED UPON BY FORCES WHOSE RESULTANT IS ZERO" (*WEBSTER'S DICTIONARY*).

One secret of pain: facing pain rather than running from it diminishes its power. Some physicians say that as much as 80 percent of our experienced pain is the result of our resistance to the 20 percent of "real" pain. The Pollyanna Principle has convinced us that we shouldn't suffer; hence, when we do we feel guilt and shame. Pain is given a bad name, tranquilized and banished from polite society. We erect facades to deny the normal suffering and tragedy of everyday life and end up with the most inhuman kind of pain—an anesthetized self. Before you seek relief from pain (and opiates are a gift of God), walk calmly into its presence. You will feel alone. Breathe into the pain; relax into it. Listen to see if it has a message.

Just beneath the surface of some pain you will often find anger lurking. As long as our ancient injuries are unremembered and unforgiven, we fester with resentment and in-rage. We dare not recall the pain and so we cannot really accuse those who wounded us. But neither do we hold them innocent. We punish them silently, by withdrawal and withholding, by bearing grudges, never quite saying that they are guilty. Or we turn the repressed anger in upon ourselves, punish ourselves with a diet of guilt, illness, or failure. Or we misplace the anger and project it onto some safe scapegoat—our mate, our children, or the enemies of our country. Frozen anger is like a black hole in space, a sink into which all feelings disappear. The most hostile of all acts is to refuse to feel anything—for or against another person. Resentment is the refusal to face another with either anger or compassion.

It is difficult to allow anger to rise hot and clean, because as children we all experienced a terrible dilemma. When we were hurt or disappointed by our parents or guardians we hated those

RESENTMENT IS THE STUNTED OUTGROWTH OF IN-RAGE.

we loved, and for a moment wished them annihilated from the face of the earth. But if our hot anger destroyed them, who would take care of us? We all learned early the mistaken proposition that we cannot hate the ones we love. In fact, all love involves deep ambivalence. Hate and love are forever linked in the dance of intimacy. It is precisely those we love most who wound us most deeply. But the knowledge of the extremes of love and hate that exist within us is too traumatic. So we dampen down our passions and exist in a monotonous climate of moderate feeling.

When we recover the memory of our hopes and disappointments, the love and pain of childhood, rage rises to flood tide. For a time the anger that emerges when any repressed person or group begins to taste liberation spills over onto almost everyone. The dam breaks and the stream rages, muddy water slopping over the banks, soiling all in its path. The barely liberated strike out at anyone who reminds them of their repressors.

It takes a lot of practice before we can accurately identify the appropriate targets for our rage. But in time the stream of anger flows clean. Resentment is converted into force and rebellion into aggression in service of the chosen goals of the person.

A male friend, a forty-two-year-old doctor, recently expressed the process of the alchemy of anger well: "A few years ago, I went into therapy because I was having trouble in my marriage. I was always fighting with my wife. I soon discovered that many of my feelings were really holdovers from my relationship with my mother. I was ashamed to admit it, but I didn't feel much at all for Mother. She was still alive, but I practically never saw or thought about her. Zero. Nothing between us. Then I began to remember my childhood, and, Jesus, everything came out.

"I remembered how she tried to turn me into a little gentleman and how she punished me every time I got dirty. Once she whipped me because I killed a goddamn fly on the kitchen table. The more I remembered, the more pissed off I was—at Mother, and at all the women who had tried to control me. If any woman said anything that even vaguely felt like a put-down to me, I jumped all over her. It took about three years (one divorce and eighteen love-hate affairs) before my anger began to subside. Now I feel anger mostly when someone actually slights or tries to control me. And Mother? Well, I have begun to remember that she also did a lot of lovely things with me. There was a lot of tenderness in her, even if she was uptight about dirt."

When anger finally becomes an occasional, welcomed visitor, and we accept the inevitable ambivalent love-hate of intimacy, then the real alchemy of emotion begins. The energy of anger—the warrior energy—can be used creatively to destroy (de-structure) the defense mechanisms (the facades and masks of personality, the prison of guilt and shame) that have kept us prisoners within the civil warfare of our own psyches.

Only you can decide to convert your anger from a reactive to a creative force, to use it to destroy the structures within yourself and within society that are crippling and imprisoning. If anyone else tries to batter down your defenses, you will instinctively resist. Turn the anger against your resignation and resentment. Aggression can be used to set us free from the burden of paranoia and the continual preparation for warfare.

Beneath the anger level we come to grief, mourning, and tears. "Grief," says Alberta Szalita in *The American Handbook of Psychiatry*,

DYING IS NATURE'S WAY OF STAYING ALIVE.

may play as important a role in psychopathology as do inflammatory reactions in medicine. The inability to engage in mourning after a loss gives rise to a number of pathological manifestations . . . chronic reactive depressions, agitated depressions . . . emotional anesthesia, intractable melancholia . . . addictions, hypochondriasis. . . . Rarely if ever do patients mention difficulties in mourning as a presenting problem. Usually the bereaved complain about other difficulties, such as inability to concentrate on work, depression, disinterest in life, anxiety states, suicidal thoughts, and the like. . . . There are few psychiatric conditions that may not mask a delayed, unfinished, or absent mourning.

The ability to grieve and mourn are central to feeling alive, because life is continually lost and found. Living and dying are two words for a single process. The twinge of excitement I feel in typing this sentence involves chemical changes in my body-mind in which cells are being born and dying at the same moment. Breath is a dance of inspiration and expiration. Everything alive is dying. *Change, energy, process, growth,* our most dynamic words to describe the way in which life pushes forward, all have homogenized within them the connotation of death.

Yet we hold on. We fear and resist death. We cling to our youth, our children, our ideas, our property, our dreams. We stay in love with yesterday in order to avoid that final tomorrow. The ego, that part of the self that seeks refuge in yesterday, believes that the only good news is no news at all. The good, or bad, old days are safe enough since they are in the deathless past.

Freud found that the refusal to mourn was the root of

SOMETIMES, TEARS ARE THE ONLY SOLUTION.

depression. The sadness of loss is never acknowledged and purged by tears, and so it remains as a moribund but silent presence—a kind of "wandering Jew" exiled within the corridors of the self. The depressed cannot let go of deadening feelings and images because they will not acknowledge the reality of loss and death.

Melancholia, which has frequently been identified with chronic boredom, is described by Szalita as "the constipation of mourning." Like the more severely depressed, the melancholy are locked into an eternal circle of impotent complaints. "Three W's—of Woe, Whine, and Wail" (Szalita) prevent them from taking stock of their actual situation and doing something about it.

There is no magic trick to opening the gates of mourning. Give up. Surrender. Open your eyes. Accept the marriage of dying and living. Remember, savor, and grieve the passing of your youth, the decline of your body, the death of loved ones. Anticipate and weep for your own ending. Early Buddhism advised those seeking enlightenment to meditate in a graveyard. Christian mystics often kept a skull on their prayer desks to remind them of their mortality. Strange as these practices seem to us, they are not morbid, only strong rituals to prevent the meditator from falling into the illusions that come from the refusal to acknowledge mortality.

There is a tribe in New Guinea whose coming-of-age ritual involves the ordeal of swallowing poison. The particular type of poison used is absorbed in the esophagus but not in the stomach. If the initiate bravely gulps the poison, it immediately lands in the stomach; he is safe and is initiated into the full status of manhood. But if he hesitates and clenches against the draft of death, his throat tightens and he dies.

A SHALLOW LIFE IS SPENT AVOIDING THE GRAVE.

This enacted parable is everyone's story. If we hesitate to swallow the bitter losses time inevitably brings us, we cannot enter fully into our humanity. Depression, boredom, neurosis, melancholia are all in differing degrees the refusal to accept loss, to mourn, and to begin again. The sad-joyful wisdom of true maturity begins with our acceptance of the unacceptable inevitability of death. Few works in the twentieth century have captured this paradoxical union of surrender and liberation better than Norman O. Brown's *Love's Body*:

> *Admit the void;*
> *Accept loss forever. To lose one's own soul.*
> *Satori, when the ego is broken, is not*
> *final victory, but final defeat, the*
> *becoming like nothing . . .*
> *The obstacle to incarnation is our horror*
> *of the void . . .*
> *Creation is in or out of the void; ex nihilo . . .*
> *If this feeling of emptiness, of something*
> *without form, and void can be deliberately*
> *accepted, not denied, then the sequel can be*
> *an intense richness and fullness of perception,*
> *a sense of the world reborn.*[1]

If I had to pick the central insight on which most religious, philosophical, and psychological systems of liberation-wisdom-therapy agree, it would be this: the best of life begins after the worst of life has been accepted; happiness surprises us after we have seen that human being is rooted in the perpetually decaying humus; "blessed are they that mourn for they shall be comforted."

GOOD MOURNING TO YOU.

* * *

What is this alchemy of feeling? By what chemistry of the psyche is mourning turned into rejoicing?

Tears are the solvents of our neurotic defenses against life. Weep for the love you wanted and did not receive. Feel the sadness of all that might have been but was not. Experience deeply the tragic limitations and contradictions of your own life. And, presto, the magic begins. Quietly the three great healers begin their work. Empathy. Sympathy. Compassion. The deeper you feel for yourself, the deeper you are able to enter into the lives of your fellows. "Oh, I see now, you are like me." You also bear wounds. You are filled with loneliness and longing. You, too, are splendid and fearful, strong and weak. You feel immortal on certain spring days and despair on bitter nights.

A friend once told me: "I never understood my father until I had a son. Now, I see how difficult it is, how much I love my son and how often I say 'no' to him, reject him because I am overwhelmed or busy with my own work. I find that I have forgiven my father for 'neglecting' me. I'm not angry anymore. And I have become very close to him. When I look at my son now and feel the love and the hopes I have for him, I feel somehow joined to every father. I get physically sick when I read about parents whose kids have been killed in Vietnam. Their loneliness and fear goes right into my guts."

Empathy, sympathy, and compassion work their alchemy because they take us out of self-encapsulation and narcissism and establish our identity *with* others. From isolation to communion. Szalita says: "Suffering that is accompanied by insight and gradual emancipation from narcissistic self-involvement leads to empathy

NARCISSISM: A SINGLE I LACKS DEPTH PERCEPTION.

that, in turn, contributes to the resolution of grief. With that comes a compassionate attitude toward others and a new commitment to life."

The words themselves reveal the secret. Empathy is the imaginative projection of the self into another. Sympathy is the even deeper state of having feelings, emotions, and experiences in common. To appreciate the psychic revolution that begins the moment we feel the first stirring of sympathy for another, we need only remember the image of the bored person huddling in the solitary confinement of a self-imposed prison. Sympathy is the breakout, the liberation, the return to the world. Compassion is feeling with another, or love. The escape from boredom and the recovery of passion begins with the e-motion of com-passion.

I feel me; I feel you; I feel we. And from this comes a new commitment to life (*commit*, from the Latin word *committere*, which means "to join, to unite, to entrust, to venture, to begin").

Compassion spells the beginning of the end of boredom, because it ends our isolation. Saul Bellow says in *Humboldt's Gift:*

> For me the self-conscious ego is the seat of bore-dom . . . the single self, independently conscious, proud of its detachment and its absolute immunity, its stability and its power to remain unaffected by anything whatsoever—by the sufferings of others or by society or by politics or external chaos. In a way it doesn't give a damn. . . . The curse of noncaring lies upon this painfully free conscious-ness. It is free from attachments to beliefs or other souls.

The alternative to compassion is graphically expressed in a magazine interview with a rock star, Gene Simmons:

EMPATHY: SEEING THROUGH TWO (OR MORE) I'S.

"When I read that people someplace are starving to death, it doesn't affect me," shrugs fire-belching Kiss bassist, Gene Simmons. "That's possibly a human failing on my part," he admits. "I'd say I'm very shallow, very much involved in surface things. I'm not looking for meaning in life at all." So what is he looking for? "It comes down to a really simple thing. I like—well, it's neither vegetable nor mineral and it's smaller than a bread box." He continues: "I never really cared for steady girl friends. Cher was the first real girl friend I had. I resent the fact that when you go with someone they expect to see you all the time." Finished? No, Simmons also feels that he and his band are "slowly becoming the new American heroes."

Feeling opens us to intercourse with the world. We agree to be engaged to enter into life—for better, for worse, for richer, for poorer. There is no guarantee that by deciding to feel you will feel *better*. Only that you will feel *more*—more of everything. More despair, more hope, more struggle, more contentment, more weakness, more power. Freud said that the best therapy can promise is to help us exchange our neurotic suffering and satisfaction for real suffering and satisfaction.

When your feelings unfreeze and start to flow, on any given day you may experience your entire repertoire of e-motions: twenty minutes of boredom, five minutes of raw terror, eight minutes of searing anger, forty minutes of sadness, two hours of struggle, four hours of satisfying self-forgetful work, nine minutes of disgust, three hours of contentment, twenty-two minutes of wonder, one hour of compassion, six minutes of joy, etc.

As we move away from boredom and cease being imprisoned

EVERY DEMON IS A FALLEN ANGEL.

on the edge of Night Country, the light e-motions become more frequent and stronger. The richness of contentment, the pride of achievement, the agony of care, the surprise of joy will deepen and become more frequent as we take the risk of stepping more fully into the world of decision and purposeful action. With the freeing of fantasy and feeling, the inward-bound part of our adventure gives way to the outward-bound.

CHAPTER 13

RISK TAKING

A risk a day keeps boredom away.
—SANDOR MCNAB

The first thing you notice is that your life is getting stale around the edges. It's tedious. You are not desperate, but the routine grinds you down. Same job, same apartment, same friends, same marriage, same loneliness, same frustration. Something needs to happen. Change. It's time to take a risk. If you don't, you will sink into boredom.

"Boredom," Rollo May told me, "is a sign that the adventure, the risk, the challenge that are the positive side of anxiety are denied."

When you think about risks you might take, the adrenaline

DEATH SAID: "PLAY IT SAFE." LIFE SAID: "RISK IT."

crashes through your system like a double scotch and soda and you get a little drunk on the mixture of fear and excitement.

But what risks should you take? Should you get married, get divorced, have a baby, get a job, give up your job, invest in AT&T, spend your money on a vacation, tell your lover to leave, take up mountain climbing, go into therapy, have an affair, go back to school? How do you know the difference between being venturesome and being foolhardy?

Risk taking is risky business. You might fail or make a mistake. One day in the middle of the clickety-clack, clickety-clack of the subway you realize that you really belong where there is fresh water and clean air. You give up your job and move—only to find that the rural life is all clods and corny as Kansas in August. Or it may turn out that raising goats fills you with Dionysian joy.

A stupid risk can cost you some or all of your life. A friend of mine, who thought caution was the same as timidity, recently strapped on an Aqua-lung and took his maiden dive alone in the ocean. "It's not smart to dive alone," he was told. "I'll risk it," he said. They never found his body. Stupid risk. I miss him.

Several years ago I was walking in a busy street with Gabriel Marcel, the French existentialist philosopher. I dodged in and out of traffic like a matador, with Chevrolets making passes close at my heels. My wife, no aficionado of my style of crossing streets, said half apologetically, "You have to take risks." "Ah," Marcel replied, "but only interesting risks."

The sentence stuck in my mind, like a banderilla. What is the difference between interesting and uninteresting risks? Between superficial and profound risks? Between desperate and hopeful risks?

A LIFE WITHOUT MISTAKES IS A FAILURE.

THE APPEAL OF DANGER

When we think of risk taking, danger naturally comes to mind. Perhaps what you need to jolt you out of the doldrums is to skydive or dangle over a chasm on the north face of Everest. What is the appeal of danger in the raw, the physical adventures in which we risk life and limb?

China Galland, one of the leaders of Women in the Wilderness, an organization that runs expeditions for women, explained to me the recent feminine romance with danger: "Women have traditionally been taught to avoid danger. Men could and should have high adventure, but women were taught to withdraw at the first sign of fear. This made us timid and robbed us of the excitement that is on the other side of fear. When you face physical danger you learn that you can do more than you thought you could. You discover confidence in yourself."

Facing danger in a tangible way provides you a living parable, a laboratory, within which you can learn the art of risk taking.

Danger is an aphrodisiac. It excites us. Bullfighters and automobile racers know that the prospect of blood in the afternoon makes afternoon delight more poignant. Flirting near the edge of death is all but indistinguishable from the vertigo of love. Our best-kept secret is that we fear and desire oblivion. And why not? Orgasm, as D. H. Lawrence was fond of saying, is "a gentle reaching out toward death."

In love and other dangers, for a time, we lose ourselves, our boundaries are washed away, and we are released from the burden of self-consciousness. Caught in a fast-moving rapid, there is, blessedly, no time for thought. The animal in us takes over and we spontaneously do what must be done. In the moment of vertigo

---

DANGER HAS SEX APPEAL.

we know in a flash how competent and frail we are. We touch the edge where life and death join and then withdraw after a brief spasm of ecstasy—back into the secure boundaries of our egos. The shadow of death is the black lace that makes romance of danger.

Danger rejuvenates. We love it because it promises to sweep away all that is old and tired in us, purge us of our boredom, and baptize us into some new reality. Like a psychedelic drug, it cleanses the doors of perception, returns us to the primal purity of the senses.

Sandra McMurray, an avid rock climber, recently described a near-death experience to me: "I was on the rock for five hours. By three o'clock in the afternoon I had reached a place where I could neither go up or down. I was stuck. I grabbed what I thought was a possible handhold and a large piece of rock, forty pounds or more, came down toward me—almost in slow motion. I dodged, and it missed. By then I realized I was really in trouble, and I began to panic. My whole body started to shake. By pure force of will I made myself breathe deeply and calm down. After a few minutes I began to look around and I saw a route that I hadn't noticed before. I worked my way, carefully, to the top of the ridge. As I pulled myself onto the mesa, I let out a whoop. I got up and started running. The briars cut into my legs, but all I felt was the ecstasy of being alive and safe. The pain was delicious. . . . For several days after that experience everything seemed psychedelic. Flowers jumped out of the background. Birds' songs seemed to reach out and engulf me. I noticed every detail. And lovemaking was just out of this world."

Or listen to China Galland describe the experience of being thrown out of the boat in Lava Falls, the world's fastest navigable rapid: "We pulled out into the current, back paddling to position ourselves before being swept over the falls. Suddenly I was swept overboard. I begin to panic but realize that I'm only wasting time. All there is to do is breathe whenever possible and relax in the middle of this intense turbulence. Nothing more. Nothing less. Time balloons, full and swollen; seconds expand into minutes; there is only the gray thundering water, the constant churning and my presence of mind. I look over my right shoulder and see an immense wave that will take me under again. I take a deep breath and give over to the forces of a river gone wild, an explosion of water. Twenty-five feet over my head, the wave curls, breaks, and crashes down on me, pummeling me into the vortex of the turbulence itself. Down, around, until the next moment, tossed up like a pebble to the surface again.

"I am through the rapid. It has all happened within forty-five seconds. . . . The intensity leaves me stripped, vulnerable, and bare. I feel transparent like a child, unable to disguise my feelings. The pounding of my heart vibrates through my entire body. I am safe, I am alive, there are friends holding me, laughing. I shake my head as though waking from a dream and let out a loud 'Whoopeee!' How good to be alive!"

Jim Peterson, *Playboy* adviser and motorcyle racer, offers an eloquent testimony to the erotic properties of danger. "Adrenaline is God's own love potion. In a race you learn to read your adrenaline and depend on it. Gradually you transfer risk into calm. The faster you go, the more things slow down. After a day on a racetrack you know every bump and turn and crack on a road. You get so you can say a leisurely hello to a jackrabbit when you are passing at 95 mph. What was at first a blur at 140 mph becomes a series of familiar details. You go into a second-gear

---

D/ANGER IS ROUGH STUFF.

clarity. The risk you are taking becomes a knowledgeable risk rather than a blind risk."

Danger makes us feel intensely alive. On the life-death edge we meet our freedom and our mortality. It is intoxicating to realize the power of choice.

THE DANGER OF DANGER

But wait a minute before you rush out to embrace danger in the raw. Maybe you should throw caution to the winds and try something more adventurous than jogging. But first let's take a look at the danger of danger. How much does it enrich and how much impoverish life? Strong medicine should be taken with caution. Psychologists have recently done studies on persons who engage in high-risk sports that suggest that a constant craving for danger may be as hazardous to your health as any other form of drug addiction.

In a study of over 250 risk takers,[1] Bruce Ogilvie found that people who crave the kind of excitement available only at the outer limits of physical and emotional endurance tend to be extremely autonomous, have a will to dominate, excel in abstract reasoning, see themselves as leaders, are self-assertive, decisive, rebellious against routine, have a low level of anxiety and a high degree of emotional control. They are loners.

"This emotional detachment also manifests itself as a reluctance to offer emotional support or counsel to others," Ogilvie reported. "Social workers they are not. Their favored relationships are transitory in nature, requiring only a superficial commitment; they neither seek nor encourage deep emotional ties with others. A typical self-description is that of one female sky diver: 'I try not to

RISK FRIENDSHIP. BE DEPEND-ABLE.

let people get really, really close to me. With the job I have and jumping, I don't make a lot of friends.'"

Ogilvie finds that risk takers are "stimulous addictive, that is, they have a periodic need for extending themselves to the absolute physical, emotional, and intellectual limits in order to escape from the tensionless state associated with everyday living."

It is interesting to see that in one important aspect Ogilvie misinterprets the meaning of his own study. It is difficult to believe that persons who maintain a high degree of emotional control are loners and are emotionally detached from others, "extend themselves to the absolute physical, *emotional*, and intellectual limits." To the contrary, the addiction to danger seems to mask an inability to take the emotional risks associated with intimacy and, perhaps, the moral risks associated with social action. Stimulus addicts get hooked on their own adrenaline.

The danger of danger is that it makes us insensitive to the risks and pleasures of ordinary living. Danger is like pepper in the stew—too much overstimulates and eventually dulls the palate. The healthy nervous system is always dancing between stress and relaxation, danger and security. Overstimulation, by danger, drugs, excess entertainment, work, worry, or even ecstasy, destroys the rhythm of health. The quest for constant stimulation, far from stretching us to our physical, emotional, and intellectual limits, tends to exile us in the domain of sensation. And even the most exciting one-track life is monotonous when compared with the polyphonic possibilities of the psyche. There is a whole symphony of risks and delights to explore, more subtle than the cymbal and bass drum sounds of raw danger, risks that may be more interesting to you than hang gliding or parachute jumping.

THE MOST DANGEROUS FICTIONS OF THE TWENTIETH CENTURY HAVE BEEN CREATED BY THOSE WHO BELIEVED ONLY IN FACTS.

PSYCHONAUTS AND COSMONAUTS
RISK TAKING IN THE INNER
AND OUTER WORLDS

There is something of a conspiracy abroad by the extroverts of the world to capture the notion of risk taking for their favorite but limited forms of macho activism. The masculine ego frequently cannot believe in its own potency unless it is doing something— preferably something dangerous.

There is more than one style of courage, more than one type of risk, more than one kind of authentic self. We might make a Whitman's Sampler of human types, but for the moment let's oversimplify and reduce it to introverts and extroverts. Some live in and others live out.

The explorers of the inner world—the psychonauts—follow the advice of Socrates—"Know thyself." They dare to sit still, to *be* rather than to *do*. They stretch feeling, imagination, and commitment to relationships to the limits. It is only the unimaginative and unfeeling extrovert who demeans the perils of the inward path. Gerard Manley Hopkins saw more clearly:

O the mind, mind has mountains; cliffs of fall
Frightful, sheer, no-man fathomed. Hold them cheap
May who ne'er hung there.

It requires steady nerve and a strong heart to penetrate beneath the facade of your persona, to strip yourself of your defenses, to break through your stereotyped roles, to deal with your infantile emotions, to confront the fears of abandonment and death. Perhaps the rarest kind of human courage belongs to the few who

THE BEYOND IS DEEP IN YOU.

dare to divest themselves of illusions, look on the horror and wonder of existence with clear eyes, and undertake the vulnerable art of becoming a lover.

Dr. Frances Lowery, a Berkeley psychologist, veteran of the Peace Corps and of a solo drive across Afghanistan, captures much of the sense of the risk of the inner journey. "What is a risk for one person is not for another. For some people it's easier to jump out of a plane than to stand up in front of an audience. For me, as for many women, what is most risky (because it is most desirable) is intimacy—relationship. A cocktail party is more frightening to me than driving across Afghanistan, because all my fears come out when I am with people. As long as I am by myself I can daydream or keep busy, but nothing challenges my images of myself. I am comfortable with myself alone. But when I am with other people I am afraid that I will not get what I really want—acceptance. I am afraid I will be seen as inarticulate, ordinary, and not very bright, and I won't be loved.

"I think many women have fears, and take their greatest risks, around relationships. Traditionally we were supposed to find much of our worth and dignity in the sphere of intimacy. So many of us wonder: If I'm not good at relationships, how much of a woman am I? Many women are now taking the risks of action as they enter business and competition. But as they do they have to face the fear that they can't have both intimacy and success in a career."

In an era when women are claiming their share of the extrovert's dream, it is important to remember and celebrate the courage and power involved in the traditionally "feminine" style of being. There is no greater risk than to remain vulnerable, to keep feeling alive, to forgive, to understand, to open the heart, to

ONE PERSON'S VICE IS ANOTHER'S VERSA.

care, to nurture growing things, to humanize the hardened face of fact with the soft unguents of poetry. (Heidegger said, "Poetically we dwell on the earth," i.e., there is only "dwelling" and earthiness where there is poetry.)

The risks of the extroverted life—the cosmonaut's adventure— are equal to those of the psychonaut. We may find or lose ourselves in action as well as in introspection. You may find fulfillment in your work. Or you may find that inch by inch you have lost any real contact with your most intimate feelings, values, and dreams as you have compromised and tailored yourself over the years in order to gain "success." Creating a house, a farm, a business, a work of art are worthy risks as long as what you are creating emerges out of your own dream and sense of purpose.

In fact, every person is both extrovert and introvert and thus there is always a time for doing and a time for being, a time to act and a time to sit quietly and try to understand. Whether you need the risk of raw danger, aggressive action, or silent vulnerability will depend on who, when, and where you are. In primitive societies, when boys reached adolescence they had to face some ordeal to win their manhood—endure pain, kill an enemy, capture a wild animal, fast. For some people the encounter with physical danger still seems a necessary part of coming of age, as well as a periodic stimulant.

At the onset of maturity we take the risk of choosing a career, getting married, or not, involving ourselves in the political agony of our time. In old age, when our energies decline and we cannot act so vigorously, we face the more imminent danger of disease and death. Whatever your situation, there is a strategy for separating the interesting from the uninteresting risks, for discovering the most significant risks that *you* might take.

YOUR DEEP DESIRE IS STILL ASLEEP. DO SOMETHING DANGEROUS. WAKE UP.

STEPS IN CREATIVE RISK TAKING

1. Find out what you *want*. Sounds simple, doesn't it? But it's not. The psychological revolution that began with Freud is based on the discovery that much of our motivation is unconscious. We often act (or rather re-act) without any awareness of what is driving us. You may be the last one to know what you *really* want. It requires a heroic adventure, a descent into the depths of yourself, to discover your true desires. For a while you will be confused. You won't want what you used to "want" and you won't yet know what the desire is that animates you. For a time you will have to leave the ordinary world—of shoes and ships and sealing wax and cabbages and kings.

Why?

Every culture is a conspiracy to convince its members to conform their desires to what is considered "right" and "good." Good capitalists compete and consume. Good Communists don't (in theory!). If you want to see how desire is manufactured, watch the propaganda that permeates closed societies or the advertising that saturates open societies. The billion-dollar advertising industry is based upon simple premises: (1) human beings are filled with longing, (2) they don't know what would really satisfy them, (3) they can be convinced that what they want is Brand X, Y, or Z. In a consumer society we are always buying the fugitive satisfaction of an obscure dream. Since we are ignorant of our deepest wants, the media superimpose their pictures of the good life on our minds, convince us that we will be happy if only we drive, drink, and dress in the "right" style (which, of course, changes constantly). In American society, to a frightening degree, we have shrunk desire to consuming, copulating, and com-

---

YOU CAN NEVER GET ENOUGH OF WHAT YOU DON'T WANT.

peting. The proverb to the contrary, we act as if we could buy happiness.

To ask the simple question "What do I really want?" is not merely risky, it is revolutionary.

2. To find out what you want, step back into your *wishes*. Set your fantasies and dreams free and let your imagination roam.

Many wishes are fleeting. They have a half-life of a few seconds. For a moment I may wish I were a cat. In a flash of anger I may wish my lover were dead. (She smiled, and I resurrected her three seconds later.) But our deepest wants are connected with those fantasies that endure. If you wish every day for four years that you could have a baby, the chances are you really want a baby. Enjoy your casual fantasies and let them vanish into oblivion. But if you consistently daydream about being a lawyer, you are touching some deeper intentionality of yourself. And wants are higher in the hierarchy of desire than mere wishes.

There is a greater risk involved in getting in touch with wants than in merely playing with passing wishes. Fantasies and dreams are disposable and may remain private. But wants represent intentions that must eventually become public and hence may bring you into conflict with people who have contradictory wants. If you really want to move to Santa Fe and he just loves St. Louis, there is going to be trouble. If you are sixty-five and discover that you have always really wanted to climb Mt. Whitney, and instead you climbed the corporate ladder, you may have resurrected a sleeping want only to have to face the disappointment of realizing that long ago you betrayed an important part of yourself. We often do not risk allowing our true wants to emerge into consciousness, because we fear the conflict

A PERSON WITHOUT OUGHTS IS LIKE A BODY WITHOUT AN IMMUNE SYSTEM.

they will cause or the sadness we will feel when we must recognize how many years we squandered in conforming and being ruled by the demands of others.

3. What are your oughts, your values? We all carry a burden of infantile oughts and secondhand values that saddle us with guilt and shame. Jettison as much of that baggage as you can. But replace the infantile with mature values. It is well to remain in touch with your wildest and most salacious wishes and wants, but what you desire must be in dialogue with what you feel *you* should do in order for your life to be rich with dignity and meaning. The most foolhardy of all risks is to abandon your sense of what is right in order to pursue what is merely expedient or pleasurable. One way to clarify your values is to imagine that someone is writing your biography. The final chapter is devoted to the contributions you made to those around you and to a celebration of your virtues. What would this chapter say?

4. Play with alternative futures. Make up a scenario for each of your wants in which you see and smell yourself in the middle of a new situation. Flesh out your most persistent fantasies. Picture yourself with a baby. Or as the leader of an archaeological expedition to Peru. Dwell on the details. Who changes the diapers? Who digs the trenches? You will find that the more concretely you imagine some desired future, the more you will be able to determine what you really want and don't want.

5. Make a calculus of risks. Mature risk taking involves calculating the probable outcomes of your proposed actions. Of course, you can never know for certain what will happen if you have an affair, or give up your job and go back to school, but it is better to weigh what might happen than it is to make a blind, impulsive decision. What do you stand to gain? To lose? What

WHAT ARE THE ODDS THAT YOU'LL BREAK EVEN?

other people will it affect? How desperate, or calm, is your need for change?

6. Locate your fears. If a realistic assessment shows that a fear is irrational and the risk is low, walk, don't run, toward it. Sometimes fear is a warning light on a shoal where you might shipwreck. But often it is a beacon light on the far shore of your unknown self. Don Juan says, "Fear is the first enemy of the man of knowledge." If you run from it you will never achieve personal power. Walk steadily into the face of your fear of public speaking, making a fool of yourself, being abandoned, flying, sex, success, commitment. And don't forget to breathe deeply. You will find that often the sensation you identified as fear was only repressed excitement.

7. Practice over a net. No aerialist trying to learn the triple somersault risks it without a net. When you are contemplating making major changes in your life, it is best to allow your decision to ripen slowly so that you have time to listen to all the wishes, wants, and oughts within yourself. Instead of rushing into a divorce, try separation. Before you sell everything and start to sail around the world, take a leave of absence, charter a boat for two months, and sail to the islands.

In order to gauge the depth of your dissatisfaction and thus your need for radical change, try changing your own attitudes and habits before you tackle major renovations. Maybe a change in the routine is all the tonic you need to revive your spirits. Vary your sleeping times. Change your diet. Stop your major addiction for a month (sex, drugs, sugar, tobacco, TV, reading, bitching, jogging, praying—whatever) and you will notice surprising changes in your energy level and perceptions. The world looks entirely different when you give up the tit of addiction. See how

WHAT YOU SEE IS WHAT YOU GET. CHANGE YOUR EYES.

much change you can instigate merely by taking the risk of talking straight. Say what you mean, soft and clear. Express your feelings. Practice listening. Very often small changes in your communication patterns will make large changes in your relationships.

8. De-cide (from the Latin *decidere,* "to cut off"). Until this point you have been playing with risk. Now it gets serious. It's nearly time to commit yourself to action. The knife is in your hand. Plato said a good philosopher carves nature at the joints. A good decision maker, like a master pruner, must cut away what is old and moribund to make way for new growth. Every real decision is a risk in which we give up something we want in the hope of getting something we want even more. I had to put the dream of being a rancher to death in order to become a writer (herding words into parentheses, sentences into paragraphs, rounding up ideas). Decide to have a child, abandon the diaphragm, and you may irrevocably change the shape of your future. Exciting and terrifying!

A vivid life, like a good painting, is created by the love of limits. Expand your imagination beyond limits and romp in fantasy through a hundred incarnations. But contract your will and energy to become a single unique person. Risk individuation. Dare to do something definite.

9. Act. Decide and then do it. Invest your time and energy in your chosen task. No matter how vivid your fantasies or strong your feelings, you must eventually act in order to avoid that feeling of helplessness that is at the heart of boredom and depression. Action is always risky. You may fail or succeed. If you have gone through the process of clarifying your desires and have a clear notion of your values and goals, your acts will seem

CARVE A PLACE FOR YOURSELF. DE-CIDE.

adventurous to you. The sap of creativity will keep you green and willowy.

YOU BET YOUR LIFE

Before you commit yourself in action, think about the magnitude of the risks you want to face. Are you up for heroic risks? Moderate risks? Trivial risks? How much adventure, how much security do you crave? How much do you dare to dream, to hope, to struggle? If all you want is, as they sing in *My Fair Lady*, "a room somewhere, far away from the cold night air, someone to take good care" of you, you may manage to get a modest amount of security, but not much adventure. You may imprison your wishes, put straitjackets on your wants, and decide that you will settle for what's safe and average. Or you can remain alive to a dream that will stretch every fiber of your psyche until the passing wind can play its entire repertoire in you.

If you choose trivial goals, you will be rewarded with trivial satisfactions. If you give your heart to the quest for a comfortable ride, God might send you a Mercedes-Benz and nothing more. The Midas myth warns us: be careful what you want; you may get it. You want gold? Go for it! But be clear—everything, including your own flesh and blood, will turn into money.

You want wall-to-wall excitement, a turned-on, high-stimulus, fast-paced chase for the brass ring on the merry-go-round? Grab the gusto and shoot the speed. As the saying goes: live fast, die young, and make a good-looking corpse.

You want to explore the fullest possible range of human experience? Get ready for a long journey; open your imagination to impossible dreams; dare to feel—anger, grief, despair, hope,

LOSE YOURSELF IN DREAMS, AND FIND YOURSELF IN ACTION.

joy, attempt tasks that are too large for any person. Reinhold Niebuhr said: "The things most worth doing cannot be accomplished in a single lifetime." Get ready to endure the agony of creativity (the one sure antidote for boredom and depression).

Heroic risks need not be dramatic. Lewis Lapham, writing in *Harper's*, puts the case well: "Genuine risks present themselves in such ordinary ways that many people, particularly those brought up on television and generous allowances, find it difficult to perceive them or accept them as sufficiently dramatic. Everybody wants to do high deeds in Hungary, to reform the system, or dictate racial integration. Hardly anybody wants to work five days a week in a storefront on West 127th Street, teaching a class of resentful citizens the rudiments of English grammar. Neither do they want to accept the commonplace risk of marriage or any sustained relation with other people."

Martin Luther sought to dignify the heroics of everyday life by the notion that every person has a vocation, or calling, from God. Skip the theology if it doesn't speak to you, but consider the underlying idea. Listen to the voices of your psyche. What is most deeply appealing to you? What dream calls you? What task is matched to your gifts? When your conscience and your desire speak with a single voice, what is it that you want to do? The heroic risk for you is to follow your own path, whether it leads to the studio, the kitchen, the office, the boardroom, the classroom, the bedroom, the garden, the laboratory, the desert, or the high Himalayas.

In the end, of course, we cannot avoid risk. You have already done the most dangerous thing—you were born free. Every day you wager your life by what you do and what you refuse to do. Each person has one vote in determining the meaning of life. By

WHY DRESS IN GRAY WHEN YOU OWN A RAINBOW?

what you want and how you act you choose the values that will govern your days.

We have reached a point in human history where the stakes are high. The wheel is turning. What will it be: war, peace, comfort, security, justice, excitement, pleasure, success, faith, care, power, knowledge, love, creativity, money, community, individuality? Step right up and bet your life.

CHAPTER 14

FROM SEX TO INTIMACY

In the beginning it's all hearts and flowers, romance and fascination. Two strangers meet, quite unlikely, but as if it were meant to be. The attraction is so strong it is not difficult to believe that fate had a hand in the arrangements. Eyes play hide-and-seek; hands touch, first shyly and then in firm caress; words intertwine, making a helix of conversation; flesh wends its way into flesh, releasing the DNA of passion that forms two bodies into one. Separate individuals blend their essential unguents and in the heat of pleasure the alchemical bond is forged—I and Thou become We.

And, for a time, that old black magic holds us in its spell. We are fascinated with each other. I listen to your stories with rapt

BOREDOM IS THE NATURAL ENEMY OF ROMANCE, A PREDATOR THAT DESTROYS ILLUSIONS.

attention. You laugh at my jokes, too much. Each touch is electric. We share secrets, take forays and then expeditions into each other's erogenous zones.

Gradually the breathless novelty with its mingled fear and desire mellows into comfort. From the warp and woof of diverse histories we weave a tapestry, a shared life.

Then comes the fall. Repetition destroys romance. In the harsh light of day-by-day proximity, the illusion begins to fade. The facades fall away. The same old games reemerge. The gentleman turns chauvinist and expects to be obeyed. The fair maiden is passive-dependent, her magnolia heart conceals a manipulative will. They look at each other across the breakfast table and are locked into their mutual disappointment.

She doesn't turn me on anymore, he thinks.

He never talks to me anymore, never shares his feelings, she thinks.

Silently, each swallows the bitter, broken dreams and sinks into disillusionment, routine, habit.

It is around the issues of sex, intimacy, and marriage (and work) that the dilemmas of boredom are often encountered. In recent years marriage, fidelity, and the nuclear family have been subjected to a lot of bad-mouthing. The suspicion grows that monogamy produces monotony. TV and the movies sell us the ideal of glamorous romance and then give us an Archie Bunker view of marriage. No wonder we joke, "Marriage is a fine institution. But who wants to be committed to an institution?" (What TV, in fact, represents is not the way we actually experience marriage but how a few, mostly Los Angeles, much-divorced scriptwriters feel about marriage.)

IN/DWELLING WITH, BE CAREFUL NOT TO INHABIT, INHIBIT, EACH OTHER.

The new goals of personal "growth" and the "right to experience everything" have led many people to the conclusion that
confinement within a single erotic relationship or in a family may
be hazardous to the individual's spirit.

Of course, our rhetoric and our actions don't match. Marriage
is dishonored only in our preaching, not in our practice. By
middle age, 94 percent of adults in our culture have been married.
Eighty percent of those who divorce remarry within five years.
Sadly, as a culture we have not discovered any effective way to
celebrate, renew, and discover ongoing excitement in those forms
of intimacy we have decided to practice.

A large part of the problem of intimacy comes from the way we
think about relationships. The romantic myth, dripping as it does
with drama and the promise of constant agony and ecstasy, does
not teach us how love actually grows slowly as revelation
deepens. It doesn't teach us how honesty grows out of struggle
and respect out of fidelity to chosen bonds. The romantic view of
love sets up a false dichotomy and forces us to choose between
devilish intoxication with constant change and the deep blue,
depressing sea of matrimony. Choose

either:	or:
romance	marriage
freedom	fidelity
adventure	security
excitement	comfort
novelty	intimacy
liberation	captivity
individuality	compromise

THE BONDS OF FRIENDSHIP SET US FREE.

either: or:

passion   family
intensity   boredom

When our erotic alternatives are forced to goose-step in such artificial dichotomies, we impose a kind of inner fascism on our psyches. The majority of us marry because a life without bonding is too lonely, empty, and comfortless, but we continue to suspect that we may have betrayed ourselves:

Perhaps, if I had only been a little more together, braver, less dependent, I might have chosen the truly heroic path—riding the crest of each moment, moving from pleasure to pleasure, promising and expecting nothing beyond the fulfillment of the moment. If only I had the ruthless courage I might have avoided entangling alliances and walked away from lovers, jobs, institutions the moment they became boring.

In fact, our disillusionment with marriage and the current crisis in intimacy are inseparable from all of the other social problems that are emerging in American society. The energy crisis and the intimacy crisis are flip sides of the same coin: our addiction to excitement, movement, action. We must have intensity, change, growth, progress. We don't hold still long enough to sink roots. Moving as we do (on the average of once every five years), we regularly divorce ourselves from place, neighborhood, community. I asked an oil company executive who had moved eight times in fifteen years if this limited his friendships to people within his company. "I wouldn't say that," he replied. "I just don't have friends anymore. After a while it was too painful to say good-bye, so my wife and I just join the appropriate clubs when we move to a new community but we never really get close to

FALSE DICHOTOMIES MAKE FALSE-HEARTED LOVERS.

anybody." Our habit of divorce from persons and places is the sacrifice we make to the god of perpetual motion. We are in a hurry to be somewhere else. The machine-driven pace of our lives does not allow us the luxury of cultivating friendship, husbanding our intimacies, growing our families, tending our communities.

Marriage and family life have become scapegoats for our dissatisfaction. When the excitement of romance inevitably dies and we are no longer "turned on," we often conclude that the problem is with our marriage or with the institution of marriage.

Dr. Carlfred Broderick, professor of sociology at USC, explains our disillusionment. "Marriage doesn't make us happy," he says, "because we expect too much from it. Very few people are happy, vital, and creative all of the time. Why should we expect people who have become devitalized to have vital marriages? Of course there is pain and boredom in marriage; there is pain and boredom in life. Marriage is a way adults live together through an entire life, so it will have some of everything the human condition deals out to us. I think it is unrealistic to think of life or marriage in terms of constant excitement."

Intimacy (whether in friendship, marriage, or in the bonded relationship to a community or a piece of land) is a Rorschach. Each of us is belly to belly with the world. The way we cultivate or avoid intimacies will reflect our style of loving or fearing life. How we confront the tedium that is an inevitable part of relationships will be a mirror image of how we choose to embrace, confront, and avoid the mystery and monotony, terror and wonder of the larger world.

Let's take a look at three styles of dealing with sex and intimacy: the way of anonymous sex, of intimate enemies, and of erotic friendships.

LOVE: HERE BEFORE THERE, NOW BEFORE THEN.

ANONYMOUS SEX:
THE LIMITS OF SENSUALITY

One common way of avoiding the threat of boredom is by avoiding intimacy and limiting relationship to mutual sensual stimulation. This can be accomplished either within or without marriage.

Before we can go further, we need to pause to look at this strange notion that the ability to deal creatively with boredom and to enjoy intimacy are linked. There is a law and logic (psycho-logic) that governs the relationships of persons no less than the interaction of atoms. The first law of intimacy is: if a relationship is to deepen into intimacy it must go beyond romance or politeness, pass through disillusionment and monotony, and emerge on the far side of the boredom barrier. That deep carnal knowledge that rightly deserves the name *love*, the trusting communion that comes from knowing and being known, comes only when we penetrate beneath the facade of fascination, beneath the masks and roles that make up the personality. We must become disillusioned with the romance of personality before we begin to reveal ourselves. A life of continued stimulation and surface excitement prevents the adventure of profound intimacy.

With this law in mind, it becomes clear that many styles of relationship prevent boredom at the price of avoiding intimacy.

One common way of avoiding intimacy is the musical-beds method: keep changing partners. This may be practiced either with the patina of romance or as a pure exercise in sensual satisfaction.

Prior to the sexual revolution this was mostly practiced by men. But women are now liberated and are free to have sex without

WHAT DO YOU WANT? READY-MADE EXCITEMENT? OR HOME-MADE JOY?

love, to explore sensuality without commitment. Erica Jong has proclaimed woman's right to "the zipless fuck." *Playgirl* magazine has matched *Playboy* with the centerfold of the month. And we are now all free to be sexual objects to each other regardless of sex, color, or creed.

The modern woman has won the dubious male privilege of heartless sex. Severing sex and intimacy keeps relations hip, superficial, and exciting. Playboys and -girls can concentrate on fun and games and avoid any commitments beyond the pleasure of the moment. The moment anything "too heavy" comes up, or boredom sets in, it is a signal to go on to the next relationship.

Ah, but problems arise. First is the increasing danger of AIDS, herpes, and an unholy host of new sexually transmitted diseases. But even aside from such major terrors, the continual stimulation of sexual variety condemns us to the very thing we are trying to avoid. Sex without care is one-dimensional. Sensory exploration is exciting but limited. When feeling is sacrificed to sensation, two persons agree to treat each other as mere bodies, to touch the surface but not to deal with each other's hopes, dreams, disappointments, injuries. Care-less lovers make a futile effort to fill an emotional and volitional vacuum with a feast of sensation.

It is becoming increasingly clear that the "sexual revolution" has been a mixed blessing. It brought much-needed relief from Victorian inhibitions and the double standard. It dissolved false guilt and shame. But it appears to have freed sex at the cost of trivializing it. Sex became the number one thrill. Unfortunately, it didn't work for long. We overlooked the obvious. It is not genitals that make love, but persons. To reduce sex to the level of pleasurable sensations turns the participating persons into interchangeable bodies.

SINK ROOTS AND SOAR.

The inevitable alienation that is created by too much anonymous sex is evident in pornography. Pornography is supposed to stimulate, but for the most part it dulls the imagination. Spend a week of evenings sampling your local porno movies and a single question emerges: Why are porno movies so unimaginative, so unartistic? With the rare exception of films like *Behind the Green Door*, most pornographic films have all the dramatic intensity and artistry of *The Hereford Breeders Guide to Artificial Insemination*. The same faceless actors and actresses go through the standard acrobatic simulations of passion. If you've seen one, you've seen them all. There are few more powerful moral sermons illustrating the virtues of keeping sex and tenderness together than the average pornographic movie!

Where sex is not an open door to a person-to-person meeting, it rapidly becomes mechanical. (Did you ever notice how many sex manuals read like *A Beginner's Guide to Genital Engineering*? Consider the angle of thrust, depth of penetration, level of arousal, rate of stimulation, management of climax, and signals of lubrication.) Screwing is boring (*bore*, "to pierce especially or as if by means of a rotary tool"). When we reduce the mystery of the phallus to a tool for making out and the generative wonder of the female to a piece of ass, the machine has crept inside our minds and bodies.

INTIMATE ENEMIES: THE BATTLE BETWEEN THE SEXES

The "battle between the sexes" is a dominant metaphor coloring our perception of relationships. Sex is often warfare and conquest.

SKIN TOUCHING SKIN. DEEP MEETING DEEP. IN SEX WE TURN INSIDE OUT.

Many of our popular sex manuals teach the techniques of seduction and conquest as if sex were a matter of strategy. In *Sex and the Single Girl*, Helen Gurley Brown tells women that men are the enemy and that being sexy is a woman's greatest weapon. Albert Ellis in *Sex and the Single Man* tells men to observe the traits of the woman he wants to win and plan an appropriate campaign to bed her. We are so dedicated, unconsciously, to seeing sex as a power struggle that we define male adequacy as "potency" (i.e., powerfulness) and female sexuality as "surrender." Sex is flowery combat. Lovers are "intimate enemies" (George Bach).

Look at the intimate relationships around you and it isn't difficult to imagine that much of what goes under the name of love is really civil war. I sometimes fear the cynic's definition of love is correct: "Love is keeping someone near enough to hit when you are frustrated." At best an uneasy peace exists between men and women. We exploit, suspect, blame, and defend ourselves against each other as if we were members of alien species.

Marriage becomes tedious when two people are stalemated. He advances, she retreats. She advances, he retreats. The distance between them remains the same. On good days they edge toward intimacy. Lovemaking is tender, they soften toward each other. Then, as if they had gotten too close for comfort, the fighting, withdrawal, and distancing begin. He criticizes her; she harbors silent resentment and becomes sexually unavailable. He threatens; she retreats further, etc.

The approach-avoidance, intimacy-fighting pattern that governs many relationships has certain advantages. Fighting brings drama. Anger frequently dispels depression. To live on an interpersonal battleground may be exhausting, but it is not boring. The good thing about fighting with those you love is that

FLESH IS SPIRIT INCOGNITO.

it keeps them strange, dangerous, and exciting; the bad thing is that it turns them into enemies and the trust level drops.

It takes patience and care to get beyond the style of intimate warfare. Trust emerges only when it has become safe for us to be vulnerable to the other. Each of us has an inner sanctum we defend as if our life depended on it. We guard a secret wound— our fear of abandonment. No matter how successfully we have created a personality with which to deal with the outside world (what Wilhelm Reich called "character armor"), within the privacy of the self we know we are terribly vulnerable. Death or tragedy can strike at any moment. Old wounds make us fearful of trusting. No one of us has been loved as well as we wish. Our hopes have been shattered too often. As long as we do not fully trust, we remain guarded. Paranoia colors all of our interactions. We perform, pretend, persuade, but we do not reveal the tender feelings that are hidden beneath our facades.

THE BOREDOM BARRIER

We begin to edge toward the possibility of true intimacy and erotic friendship when we agree to confront our boredom.

Relationships inevitably reach boredom because they begin as the meeting of mask and mask, role and role, archetype and archetype. In the beginning, we usually repeat the patterns of male-female relations that have been imprinted on us by our parents and society. We expect our mates to act the way husbands or wives "are supposed to." As novices in relationship, we can't help seeing the world through Mother- and Father-tinted glasses. We repeat the old patterns unconsciously, have the same fight

---

BOREDOM IS AN INSTANT REPLAY. DÉJÀ VU.

time after time. ('I'm tired of being the one who always initiates sex. Why don't you be more aggressive?')

But when we become conscious of our unconscious ways of relating, something new emerges. Noticing your stereotyped acts is the beginning of creative intimacy. Instead of my having to be 'the man' all the time (aggressive and thrusting) and you 'the woman' (nice and receptive), we begin to play, to change roles in the hay, and move toward erotic friendship.

THE ART OF EROTIC FRIENDSHIP

Before we examine the art of becoming friends with your lover, or vice versa, let's step back and look at the problem in a larger context. The difficulty of combining passion and commitment is not new. Freud noted that the incest taboo is responsible for a normal splitting off of feelings of sexual passion and tender caring. When our erotic feelings first emerge in childhood, we are taught that it is inappropriate to feel attracted in a sexual way toward our parents or siblings. ('It's just *not* done in the best of families.') From the beginning, our sexual feelings are directed toward persons who are unfamiliar. We are supposed to love proper strangers, not people with whom we are already intimate.

The prohibition against incest is frequently unconsciously extended to include anyone with whom we have deep friendships. A friend *feels like* a member of the family—therefore taboo. Intimacy gets confused with incest. If this unconscious—but natural—confusion is not brought to the surface and dealt with on a conscious level, we will experience panic every time we approach intimacy. As soon as a man begins to love a woman, at some primal level she becomes Mother; he fears incest and must face the forbidden feeling of sexual excitement toward a woman who also arouses his feelings of tenderness. When a woman loves and respects a man, he will take on some overlay of emotions connected with Father. When these unconscious attractions and repulsions are not brought into awareness, romantic affairs tend to be a frustrating dance of approach and avoidance, advance and retreat. Sex will be good until friendship begins to develop. Or vice versa.

Maturity involves learning to create relationships in which there are both excitement and comfort, sex and caring, spontaneity and continuity. But relational maturity doesn't just happen. It is an art and a significant achievement to create an erotic friendship. And it doesn't usually happen when we are in our teens or early twenties. For good reason. In our teens and twenties we need to explore different types of relationships to discover what is and is not satisfying. Puppy love and early romances teach us that pure romance lasts about ninety days and is not a good basis for a lasting relationship.

Many people also seem to need to get a bellyful of sex without love before they become convinced that it's better with love. And it often takes several "serious" relationships for most of us to lose the illusion that if we can just find the right person we will live happily ever after without any conflict. In short, we have to play a lot of erotic games (Conquest and Seduction, Someday My Prince Will Come, Musical Beds) before we gain enough experience to get down to the rewarding work of turning enemies, strangers, and lovers into friends.

The following guide to the art of erotic friendship is relevant only to those who have grown weary of the battle between the sexes. If you are tired of sex without intimacy, or vice versa, here are some principles to explore.

DON'T GET ATTACHED TO YOUR PERSONALITY.

* * *

Rise above the battle. Become an observer of the way conflict keeps you in the stance of enemies. Learn to say to each other without rancor: this way of deciding issues, making love, dividing household responsibilities, entertaining friends doesn't work; let's try something new.

Conspire with your friend to have it all. Help each other stretch your potentials to their fullest. Use the channels you normally neglect: enjoy sensation, express feeling, play with imagination, clarify values, take the risk of action. At one end an erotic friendship is a private sharing of the pleasure of sensual and sexual touch; at the other end it is a shared purposefulness that is expressed in action in some tangible way—making a home, a child, working a farm, creating a business, taking political action, traveling, building something together. The most exciting friendships are those in which two people encourage each other's growth and movement toward greater wholeness.

Change roles. Break stereotypes. The pattern of big-daddy-taking-care-of-little-girl is a fine variation as long as you can switch and be little-boy-being-held-by-mother. Learn to be parent, playmate, provocateur, companion. Everyone needs to learn to be tough and tender, emotional and rational, spontaneous and disciplined, thrusting and surrendering. A complete person is able to practice both masculine and feminine virtues. The ability to change sexual roles doubles your pleasure. On any given day or night, switch positions. It doesn't matter who is masculine or feminine. Both are lovely melodies. It is the duet that counts.

Examine your attitudes toward sex. The point of this activity is to make love, not war. How much are you still hooked on conquest or performance? How willing are you to divorce sensation from affection? How much knowledge and trust of the other do you need before you feel comfortable with sex? In erotic friendships, sex is an expression of a union, a celebration of a meeting that has already taken place. Don't start making love until you have already come together. Sexual love is an invitation to the second coming. Let sexual sensations be explored within a context of feeling and care. In making love, the trick is to begin at the end. Start when compassion has already been established.

Take your time. Intimacy is not created in a night. Our Instamatic culture seduces us into the dangerous illusion that everything can be done in a hurry. You may tell the anonymous stranger on the plane secrets you would not normally reveal, but that is because you won't see him again. True friendship is woven from a thousand shared days, from the accumulated yarn of memories and hopes. It only happens when you have shared a lot of stories. Speed is the enemy of intimacy; love cannot be prefabricated.

You and I put out tendrils toward each other. In the beginning, everything is tentative. Gradually our roots intertwine and a bond is formed. You know it is beginning to happen when you stop saying "You" and "I" and begin to say "We."

MAYBE THE UNKNOWN IS BETTER THAN ANYTHING YET KNOWN.

*   *   *

Learn to trust. In the beginning is mistrust. It is normal and even wise to be hesitant and reserved with strangers. But we only learn to trust if we are willing to admit that we are suspicious and perhaps untrustworthy. Overcoming paranoia is a universal human task. Other people, especially those of the opposite sex, are unknown and dangerous until proven safe. All of us have been exploited, rejected, and abandoned enough by the time we reach our adult years to have cause for suspicion. And too many broken romances and disappointed hopes lead automatically to a hardening of the heart.

Trust is always a risk. But it is the only path toward intimacy. How much of yourself do you withhold because you are fearful of being used or abandoned? How much suspicion and free-floating hostility do you have about men in general? About women? Paradoxically, one way to deepen trust is to confess to another that you would like to trust but are unable to. Trust your friend enough to share your mistrust. The more we are able to be open in a relationship about our fear, envy, guilt, grief, hopes, the more trust grows. In a mature friendship, two people are able to tell each other precisely in what ways they are untrustworthy. "I warn you, I have a lot of anger toward men, and some of it will spill over on you." Or, "I am still terrified of commitments."

Expand your friendships. Avoid the romantic trap of imprisoning yourself in a single intimacy. When two people gaze only at each other, they become myopic. All your intimacy needs cannot be satisfied by a single friend. An erotic friendship is an opening relationship.

What about sex with other friends? It is always the number one question in open relationships, and there are no easy answers. For many people, the sexual bond is exclusive. Very few "open marriages" survive for long. Anxiety and jealousy and constant negotiations eat away the trust and comfort that is the foundation of friendship. Rare couples can tolerate and encourage plural sexual relationships. Only you and your lover can decide. Is your friendship bond strengthened or weakened by including others within your sexual intimacies?

Virginia Satir advises couples: "You must be as free to be closed as you are to be open."

It is unfortunate when the question of plural friendships gets hung up on the matter of genital expression. Modern America is a lonely society; most of us have many acquaintances and few friends. We desperately need to renew the art of friendship. In one American Indian language, "monotony" is defined as "an absence of male friends." Interesting! When men do not have friends, they place all of their emotional needs on a single woman or series of women. This usually puts such pressure on the relationship that it cracks under the strain. Women's Liberation made women sensitive to their needs for other women. Most men have yet to learn the deep satisfaction of relating to each other in a noncompetitive, trusting, and tender way. Fortunately, the men's movement is now demonstrating men's need for male friendship.

THE GREAT ADVENTURE BEGINS WITH THE QUEST/ION OF WHAT'S MISSING FROM YOUR LIFE.

* * *

Beware of sexualizing your need for adventure. We try to
make up in sex for the excitement that is missing in our lives. If
you are obsessed with the question "How can I, or we, have an
exciting sex life?" you are probably focusing on the wrong
question. Discover a "path with heart," a guiding passion for life
that you share with your lover, and your level of sexual excitement will rise. Continued sexual excitement in a relationship is
the result of a joint pursuit of an adventurous way of life.

Reveal yourself. Friendship deepens with self-revelation. Each
step requires a further risk. Disarm. Lay aside your defensiveness,
your pretenses, your cultivated images of self. It's both dangerous
and exciting, because there is no place to hide. Friends see
through all sham. And it is hard to be honest. But within
the sanctuary of trust we may put aside the competition and polite
warfare that govern the ordinary social world and allow ourselves
to be known.

Make a commitment. Art requires discipline. Freedom begins
with self-limitation. For every friendship we develop, several
potential relationships must be sacrificed. It takes time and energy
to cultivate a friendship. As the old song says: "If you call
everybody darling, then love won't come a-knocking at your
door." That special thing will remain special only if you share it
with those who are special to you. Milton Mayeroff says it well:
"Caring assumes continuity and is impossible if the other is

FREEDOM IS: THE DECLARATION OF INTERDEPENDENCE.

constantly being replaced."[1] Love grows only in a climate of promise and loyalty.

Learn to depend and be dependable. Many modern Americans suffer from an Atlas complex—the illusion that they can support the world on their shoulders. The Marlboro man and the totally independent woman are committed to a false autonomy. When someone says, "I don't need anybody," it is merely a disguised way of saying, "I am afraid to trust." Pseudo-independent people live in a world of isolation and loneliness rather than risk the loss of a tenuous sense of self. Human beings are relational animals. We need each other. It is a strength rather than a weakness to be aware of our need to care and be cared for. Examine your fear of "losing your freedom," your discomfort with needing others. Risk becoming interdependent.

Cultivate privacy and solitude. Here is a paradox of passion: the greater the intimacy, the greater the need for solitude. In profound love affairs, we merge and lose ourselves. The boundaries between I and Thou are erased and we are moved by a common impulse. After such mergers we need to reestablish our separate identities. Couples who do not understand this need for oscillation between blending and separation get the necessary distance by fighting, withdrawing, or going into periods of emotional frigidity. A strong relationship, like breathing, is a rhythmic flow—in and out, coming together and moving apart,

LEARN TO BE ALONE TOGETHER.

interdependence and solitude. Allow emptiness. Don't exhaust each other by unbroken togetherness.

Keep open to the strange, the unknown mystery of your most intimate friend. Do not allow yourself to slip into the assumption "I *know* her completely." Expect to be surprised and you won't be disappointed.

Pursue your lover's well-being. Become a connoisseur of growth. Use your insight to encourage him/her to become who he/she is. Learn to criticize without blaming and appreciate without flattering. There is nothing more erotic than watching another human being blossom, unfold, and grow ripe with the years. Respect is a great aphrodisiac.

In summary, it is not an impossible dream to join passion and tenderness, to find a lover and a friend in the same person. In theory, it's easy:

Free your sexuality from conquest and performance.

Cease being a warrior and become a lover.

Destroy your paranoia and become vulnerable.

Learn to trust, accept disappointment, forgive, and trust again.

Face your fears of abandonment and other impediments to intimacy.

Enjoy your body; delight in your lover.

Honor your needs for belonging and solitude.

Express yourself honestly.

THE ONLY SOLUTION IS LOVE.

Take responsibility for your own growth.
En-courage and care for your friend.
Share time, stories, hopes, failures.

In practice, it takes just about a full lifetime to perfect the art of loving. But you get better at it every year. And I can't think of any more valuable way to spend a life than learning to be a friend and a lover.

CHAPTER 15

THE POLITICS OF DEPRESSION AND HOPE

If depression and melancholy were rare as tuberculosis, we might have ended this book with the consideration of the cure of the individual psyche. A decade ago, 32 percent of women and 16 percent of men in the prime of life (30–44) (NIMH statistics) were using prescription drugs for "mood elevation," between 9.3 and 10 million adults and 3.3 million teenagers were classified by HEW as problem drinkers. The recent explosion of twelve-step programs and the recovery movements lead me to suspect that all forms of addiction are more pervasive in the nineties than they were in the eighties. Something more than personal psychological maladjustment is involved.

EACH PSYCHE IS A CELL IN THE BODY POLITIC.

To discover the causes and cure for our disease, we have to go beyond psychology to the politics of boredom.

The thesis of this chapter is unorthodox and controversial: the epidemic of boredom and depression is a symptom of cultural rather than individual failure. Those who are bored and depressed may be *superior* rather than *inferior* to "normal" Americans who can carry on business as usual in this time of cultural crisis. It is the most sensitive among us who are overwhelmed by the mechanization, standardization, militarization, bureaucratization, urbanization of modern life—our cultural dis-ease.

There is much that is depressing in modern America (and Europe, and Russia, and China). Our private feelings of melancholy are a warning that we are in danger of destroying the relationships, the communities, the institutions, the fabric of ecology, without which we cannot survive on this planet. We are depressed because we are walking deeper and deeper into helplessness.

How does our culture depress us? What changes must we make to chase the blues away from our body politic?

These questions, obviously, require answers too large to be squeezed into a chapter. But let's dip into American culture at four points (women, work, TV, war) to sample some of our problems and possibilities.

WOMEN'S WISDOM

First, let's listen to women. If there is wisdom to be gleaned from depression, much of it will have to come from getting more deeply in touch with our feminine sensibilities.

In America, women are, in the words of Maggie Scarf's article,

---

DEPRESSION IS LIVING IN A BROKEN-PROMISED LAND.

"The More Sorrowful Sex"[1] Between two and six times as many women as men are diagnosed as suffering from depression. Seventy percent of mood-altering drugs are taken by women. Why? Women go to doctors more often than men, and most doctors are men. Hence there is a tendency to label women who are unhappy and frustrated as "depressed" and get rid of them by prescribing a drug. Since "85 percent of those who use mood-altering drugs report that they had never seen a psychiatrist" (Scarf), it is clear that much of the labeling of depression *and the implicit interpretation of its meaning* takes place in the physician's office.

The physician sees a woman who is complaining of vague distress; he finds nothing organically wrong; he decides (without the benefit of psychological training or philosophical reflection on the significance of melancholy) that she is suffering from depression; he prescribes the only cure he knows—drugs. And thus, woman's pain has been judged the result of some failure to adapt, her agitation tranquilized, and hope is offered to her in the form of a magic pill that will alter her "mood." Mood indigo disappears, and with the help of Librium she soon feels back in the pink (which is where good little girls belong).

Ms. Scarf suggests that women are more depressed than men because they are taught to be more dependent and affection-seeking, and thus they rarely achieve an independent sense of self. "Woman gives her highest priorities to pleasing others, to being attractive to others, to being cared for, and to caring for others. . . ." Women receive ferocious training in a direction that leads away from thinking "What do *I* want?" and toward "What do *they* want or need of me?" The result of this is that when important relationships collapse and there is a time of interpersonal drought, "the normally feminine, normally dependent woman may experi-

We are. Therefore, I am.

ence her inner world as emptied of what is good and meaningful to her." The depressed woman has lost something upon which she vitally depends—the love bond.

From this picture of depression of modern women, two nonchemical paths of hope diverge.

The first way is toward greater power, individuation, and liberation. Many women have been liberated from old roles. Women's Liberation has helped women jettison helplessness and dependency and marshal their aggression and demand a just piece of the economic and political pie. Many have answered Henry Higgins's question—"Why can't a woman be more like a man?"—by showing they can compete, conquer, and command as well as the best of men. As women have pushed their way into the formerly masculine roles, they have begun to enjoy the privileges of power and, in equal ratio, the stress.

The second way is more radical and exists only as a future possibility: change culture rather than women; bring what has been considered the feminine element into full equality. This radical alternative rests on an interpretation of the significance of the psychic pain and melancholy that a large proportion of contemporary women are feeling.

Let's suppose for a moment that there is something unique in what we have called the feminine mode of seeing and being in the world; and, although some men have it and some women don't, the majority of women in our culture still are the primary bearers of feminine vision. Let's further suppose that this mode of being has not been fully honored in our male-dominated, technological, left-brain, rational, activistic, competitive culture. And finally, let's suppose that the depressed among us might be prophetic and not sick.

INVEST IN LOVE BONDS.

Depressed women may be sorrowful because at some deep, intuitive level they understand that we are in danger of losing precisely those attitudes, feelings, values, and behavior without which human life cannot survive. Perhaps woman's pain is cognitive, accurate, true! The most neurotic among us may be those who do *not* get depressed when the love bond is threatened, who harden themselves to "get along" without caring or being cared for.

There is a nearly forgotten tradition that sorrow is the gateway to the authentic human condition. In both Judaism and Christianity, the expected Messiah—the one who was to lead us into the new reality—was "a man of sorrows and acquainted with grief." Deep sorrow marks the awareness that something we love and value is threatened or has died. It is only by mourning the old that we can move out of depression and create a new future.

I suggest that the epidemic of depression among women is a signal from deep within our collective DNA that we are in trouble. The melancholy of our time may be a healing dis-ease, a wound that forces us to change the trajectory of our individual and political lives.

What is woman's voice telling us? What are the words that go with the blues?

In the beginning is love, intimacy, bonding.

The matrix that unites mother and child is only one junction of the nexus of cosmic communion within which we live and move and have our being.

"We" comes before "I." Communion is prior to individuality.

The giving and receiving of care is the humus in which our humanity will always be rooted.

IF YOU'RE NEVER SAD OR ANGRY, YOU DON'T UNDERSTAND WHAT'S HAPPENING.

Without feeling, touch, and familiarity we become aliens in our own land, alone and afraid.

The family and the community and the land are the cradle of hope. Children are hope incarnate, our living future.

Women's consciousness seems to be centered in the awareness of relationship. Increasingly, biology, physics, and ecology demonstrate that all reality is relationship. Women, it seems, have a dogged grasp on the real. In its depths the feminine psyche has never accepted the modern experiment in individualism with its ethic of "I do my thing, you do your thing, if we happen to meet, okay, if not, too bad." It has never believed that everybody can take care of him- or herself. It has never believed the abstract was more important than the concrete, the marketplace more valueful than the hearth, or the remote more worthy of allegiance than the proximate. It has never fallen under the illusion that the accumulation of power is the aim of life.

If woman bears a genetic urgency to create relationship, to care, to nourish the bonds of family and community, how could she not feel pain and discouragement in present society? The deterioration of family and community, the pollution of the earth, and the looming horrors of war eat away at our belief in the viability of the future. Sociologists have diagnosed widespread alienation, anxiety, anomie. We increasingly live fast, high, and anonymous. We are well-fed but lonely, entertained but bored; we have sex a lot but are seldom loved.

Woman's melancholy cry calls to us to change our priorities, to reorder our economics and politics, to move beyond competition and individualism toward a more caring body politic. It calls us to revere our bonds with Earth, to honor the intimacy without which we become hardened, to treasure the families that are the

DEPRESSION IS CARE/LESSNESS.

nest of freedom, to work for communities that are rich in cooperation and sharing. We usually ignore women's wisdom, because it would require revolutionary changes in our society. Our contemporary crisis comes from the growing awareness that we may have to change or die. Perhaps we are nearly desperate enough to listen to the soft wisdom we have silenced for so long.

It is a sign of hope that, at long last, men are awakening from their patriarchal dreams and beginning to reclaim their feelings and intuitions. The budding men's movement is sending thousands on the inward-bound adventure where they are discovering many of the spiritual values that women seem never to have wholly forgotten. We seem to be a generation of recovering sexists. It's time now to trust our feelings, respect our pain. Perhaps we should throw away our Elavil and Valium and start changing ourselves, our relationships, our family, our community.

WORK—FOR WHAT?

Does the monotony of work make you want to scream?

Work is a paradox. We do it and complain that we feel locked in or trapped by our jobs, yet most of us would continue working even if we did not have financial needs. Only 28 percent of us would continue working because we enjoy what we do on the job.

Why work?

If we don't work we don't eat. A majority endure jobs because they have no alternative. In a technological culture most are condemned to boredom by the demands of industry. The economic order depends on routine, standardization, regularity, quantification, and on a large laboring class whose work is

HOPE GROWS FROM CARE.

reduced to monotony. Monotony is merely another name for efficiency. Wealth is based on the mass production and sale of products. Since the primary investment of capital is in machines that must be kept busy, people must be induced to structure their lives to harmonize with the needs of the machines. People must be cut to fit the job, not vice versa. In an economic society the clock is king. Body rhythms be damned, you arrive at work, ready or not, at 8:00 A.M., eat at 12:00, hungry or not, and quit at 4:00. Manfully and womanfully we shoulder our responsibilities, commit our freshest energy to work, and endure the inevitable boredom. We have to. Or so we think.

If we look deeper, we find many other motivations for work. In a *Psychology Today* survey, those who said they would continue to work even if they had no financial necessity gave the following reasons:[2]

	Male	Female
I enjoy what I do on my job.	29%	28.6%
I derive the major part of my identity.	25.8%	27.5%
Work keeps me from being bored.	17.4%	18.2%
My work is important and valuable to others.	13.9%	10.8%
I enjoy the company of my co-workers.	5.3%	8.1%
I would feel guilty if I did not contribute to society through gainful employment.	4.4%	3.4%
I would continue out of habit.	4.2%	3.4%

The mixture of motives reflected in this survey suggests that we endure work not only because we must to survive but because it is part and parcel of the other goods we derive from working—

VOCATION: EVERY CRY IS SOMEONE'S CALLING.

creativity, identity, engagement, service, company. Like the man who discovered roast pig when his house burned down and continued the expensive habit of arson to get barbecued pork, we put up with boredom because we love to be employed.

If women have traditionally found their identity in relationship, men have discovered theirs in work. The first question a man asks another is: "What do you do?" We demand more from our work than subsistence. We want meaning and a sense that we are serving others and creating something of value. Here is the catch-22 in modern work: we continue to demand significance from work and yet our jobs are systematically trivialized by the demands of increasing mechanization, urbanization, and bureaucracy. A society devoted to production and consumption manufactures what makes a profit, not what is worthwhile.

The hidden demands we place on work are so enormous that we have a difficult time coping with the absence of work—leisure. We think we want a leisurely life, but too much free time is a greater burden than too little free time. We invest so much identity and hope in work (regardless of the satisfaction it actually gives us) that when we are denied work we hardly know what to do.

In the McCarthy era, one famous movie director at first refused to testify before the House Un-American Activities Committee and was blackballed and forced out of work. He finally gave in and testified because he was sexually impotent all the time he was unemployed. The association of job, status, and masculinity is so common that many men die soon after retirement. No work means no identity. Leisure is threat.

There are two ways out of the dilemma.

We could divorce job and vocation. You might give up any

PASSION IS DOING SOMETHING ON PURPOSE.

expectation that your job will be creative or meaningful and settle for making a living doing anything that is required. A job is for a paycheck. Your vocation, the activities in which you find meaning, identity, community, and an outlet for your creative urges, might then be exercised in creating a home, a work of art, a relationship, a hobby. We might surrender our working hours to the profit machine and keep our leisure for the pursuit of meaning.

Or we might demand that the business, shop, store, farm, union, office in which we work begin to employ us in more meaningful ways. We might demand that automobiles be safe, durable, and economical; that law offices serve justice more than legality; that schools educate rather than merely teach; that every job in some way be an opportunity to serve the public good and not merely make private profit.

No job can or should employ you fully—emotionally, mentally, spiritually—and provide you a full identity. The question you must decide is: What proportion of the meaning and satisfaction of your life do you expect your job to provide? Your friends? Your family? Your political involvement? Your play and leisure?

If you decide that your job should express a large part of your vocation and give you room for expressing some of your creative, moral, and political impulses, you may run smack into trouble. The power structure in any society is that group of persons who have the force to impose boredom on others. Saul Bellow suggests in *Humboldt's Gift:* "This combination of power and boredom has never been properly examined. Boredom is an instrument of social control. Power is the power to impose boredom, to command stasis."

BOREDOM IS DOING NOTHING, AIMLESSLY.

Are you caught in a nine-to-five rut where your working hours don't match your body rhythms and your job description doesn't make use of your creativity? When you try to change your working conditions you will discover how much or little power you have. Insist on your right to interesting and meaningful work and you risk having to revolutionize your employer or create your own job.

The specialized nature of work in industrial societies raises an even more fundamental question: Does specialization condemn us to boredom? The modern world is increasingly made up of specialists and experts who know more and more about less and less. Doctors (themselves splintered into proctologists, internists, dermatologists, etc.) take charge of our bodies; psychiatrists adjust our psyches; the clergy take care of what remains of the soul. Professional politicians govern us. Lawyers tie us up in contracts every time we marry or divorce or buy property. Agribusinessmen produce our foods.

Specialization has allowed us to create a complex society in which individual gifts and interests can find scope for expression. And individualism inevitably leads to specialization. Who can deny that the world is richer for Picasso's having the freedom to devote a lifetime to art, or Einstein to pure mathematics? But what is the price of overspecialization?

Last year I sat watching peasants come to market in a small Mexican village. All were poor by American standards, but as I watched their faces—strong and beautiful, etched with lines that told the story of years of hardship and labor—I wondered whether they were freer than middle-class Americans. Each one of them had the primal knowledge of how to survive. They could grow food, doctor their sick, make their houses. The more

EXPERTS KEEP US STRAIGHT AND NARROW-MINDED.

sophisticated our culture becomes, the fewer things the average citizen knows how to do for himself. We make money and pay experts to birth our children, make our clothes, compose our songs, play our games. Sex remains one of our few amateur activities.

In the world of specialization we are confined to a limited range of skills and delights. It may be exciting to become competent in brain surgery, but what of the person who is forced to spend a lifetime processing insurance applications? Specialization in routine jobs spells certain monotony. And anxiety. Wendell Berry identifies specialization as the central disease of the modern character. The average American, he says, has lost the power to provide himself with anything but money:

> From morning to night he does not touch anything that he has produced himself, in which he can take pride. . . . The average citizen is anxious because he *ought* to be . . . because he is helpless. That he is dependent upon so many specialists, the beneficiary of so much expert help, can only mean that he is a captive, a potential victim. If he lives by the competence of so many other people, then he lives also by their indulgence. . . . He has one chance to live what he conceives to be his life: his own small specialty within a delicate, tense, everywhere-strained system of specialists.[3]

As a society we are so governed by the specialist system that it is hard to imagine what it would be like to reclaim our lives from the control of experts. But it is not hard to imagine that we would be richer and more secure if our education included spending a

AMATEURS ARE LOVERS.

season growing food, learning the elements of health care so that we could birth our own children and take care of our own dying, building a house, fixing a car, arguing a case in court, playing music, writing a story, teaching a child, programming a computer.

It is interesting to speculate what would happen if unions began to demand more meaningful employment. What if we insisted on the right to create something of value, to contribute, to be of service, to do work that gave us pride? What would happen if the deep desires hidden in women's melancholy and men's boredom emerged as demands to change our economic and political priorities?

THE MEDIA VS. THE IMAGINATION

Is TV turning us into a nation of voyeurs whose excitement comes from watching others acting?

The evidence is growing that television is a major producer of passivity, a depressant of the imagination, a destroyer of passion—a dangerous drug. "A majority of adults in the United States currently spend more than one-half of their waking, nonworking time in front of their television receivers; the typical preschool child watches fifty-four hours a week; 99 percent of U.S. homes own a TV set, which is turned on an average of 6½ hours every day."[4]

And what is happening to us during these TV hours? No matter whether we are watching "Richard the Third" or "The Simpsons," *the TV signal itself* freezes eye motion, inhibits analytical thinking and responsive memory, and reduces us to a semi-infantile state of passive dependence not unlike that characteristic of any form of drug addiction.

ARE YOU WORTH/WHILING YOUR LIFE AWAY?

In *Four Arguments for the Elimination of Television*, Jerry Mander reviews some of the devastating evidence that is accumulating. Some of his conclusions: TV does not expand our knowledge but rather confines us within a cerebral mode; the TV signal itself produces a hypnotic-addictive effect; it inhibits learning by placing us in trancelike alpha states in which no organized thought is possible. Reading, by contrast, produces a high amount of beta-wave brain activity because we must interact with a book. TV decreases vigilance, inhibits action, creates sensory cynicism, makes hard-edged, narrow minds, programs our unconscious with secondhand dreams, destroys our appreciation of complexity, and creates a mentality that buys the commercial vision of life.

It is easy to overlook the obvious: even if TV were chock-full of high-quality programs, it would still offer us a vicarious experience of life. "Romeo and Juliet" is no substitute for the zing of adolescent kisses and the rising sap of first love; and a thousand sit-coms will never shake the flesh as much as a single, spontaneous belly laugh. Art does enrich life, but an excess of passive viewing fills us with alien dreams that we have no time to digest. Six and a half hours per day even of the classics of the human spirit would exile us from an active relationship with our own life story. The vicarious life is a substitute. The more fascinating TV becomes, the more likely we are to wake up one day and find that we forgot to live. Someone said that wealthy Victorians let their servants do the living for them. We are in danger of letting professional athletes play our games, professional soldiers do our fighting, and professional politicians do our deciding.

Our situation is close to Plato's description of the prisoners in the Cave of Ignorance. Like those prisoners we sit in a dark room and can see nothing except the shadows of images on the wall.

TV IS BOREDOM IN A BOX.

And we mistake the image for reality. ("Is there really a bionic man, Daddy?") Night after night, banal and violent dramas dance before our eyes and hypnotize our minds. The flickering phantasms become our friends. Our psychic worlds are inhabited by ghosts without flesh who make empty speeches that command our attention. Increasingly we are exiled from other people and confined to our caves, homes. (The word *idiot* in Greek signified a private person without political involvement.)

Without dreams a body and a body politic die. When we sit in silence and introspect, we get in touch with our deepest unconscious desires. In daydreams our yet-unfinished self calls to us, the promise of who we might become writes itself on our consciousness. Dreams have power to shape us. The danger of the TV age is that mediaspection is replacing introspection: prepackaged dreams programmed by merchants who want us to buy their products and propagandists who want to rule our minds destroy the silent and fertile darkness that is necessary for us to listen to the voices of our own intimate fantasies.

Whoever controls a nation's dreams holds the power to shape its reality. The image makers, fabricators of heroes and heroines, storytellers, official bards shape our desires and govern what we came to love. Once we had living bards, traveling troubadours, family picnics where uncles told you naughty things your father did when he was a boy, and grandfathers and mothers who remembered back to the beginning of time. Now, at best, we have serialized soap operas brought to you by a corporation for whom you are a carbon copy, a cloned consumer. By the images it gives and withholds, TV shapes what we desire. Gene Youngblood states the case:

A SEDENTARY LIFE IS NOT MOVING.

We can desire only what we're given. Desire is learned. . . .
It's a habit formed through continuous repetition of a
particular class of interactions. Desire is the most important
of all industrial products, acquired by enforced habit
through the absence of alternatives. So it's not only that we
can desire what we're given; what's equally significant is that
we *cannot* desire what we're *not* given. We do, of course,
make our own selections of materials with which we cultivate our personal meanings, values, and preferences. . . .
But we cannot cultivate that which is not available. We don't
order a dish that isn't on the menu. We don't vote for a
candidate who isn't on the ballot. . . . We rarely select
what's scarcely available, seldom emphasized, infrequently
presented. . . . The videosphere is populous with models
of human failure, but where are its maps of success and of
joy? How are we to live healthy lives when the videosphere
pictures only pathology and corruption? . . . The very
essence of totalitarianism is the control of desire through
the control of perception. . . . The challenge of modern
times is that of learning how to need another way of life.[5]

Much boredom in modern society comes from the artificial
limits to imagination that are imposed on us by our addiction to
media, especially TV. Our imaginations have been usurped and
colonized by the major corporations who want to turn us into
passive consumers. The existence of commercial TV depends on
your holding still, not asking questions, being obedient to the
false little messages of feigned enthusiasm the official heroines
whisper in your ear and following the advice of the cynical

VOYEURS WOULD RATHER SEE THAN BE.

"personalities" who lend their names to convincing you that Sugar Smacks are good for you. They aren't! We must be mindless or the system doesn't work. Don't touch that dial!

VIOLENCE—THE FINAL SOLUTION

The boredom of the silent majority remains largely unconscious. The void is too painful, too confusing. But it is there. How can we tell? After all, we can't photograph a vacuum. Did you ever watch what people at a party do when some unlucky person has stepped in dog shit? An invisible barrier is drawn and everyone begins to avoid the polluted area without any spoken acknowledgment that something stinks. Same with boredom. We can tell how pervasive it is by watching the lengths to which people go to avoid it.

The silent majority still prefer psychic and political violence to the specter of boredom. The tension within the body politic is between a minority who feel the blues and the majority who are red-blooded advocates of power and aggression. Red, white, and blue = anger, boredom, and depression. The reds believe we must defend the American way of life with blood. The blues see only the hopelessness of our present situation, and eat and drink to forget. Both avoid the void, the white neutral state of doing nothing, feeling nothing.

Violence is now an accepted part of the American way of life. As my wife, Jananne, says, "War is the pimple of boredom come to a head." In cold and hot wars and arms races, we spend our lifeblood in elaborate defense mechanisms. We strengthen our perimeters, toughen our resolve to spend, and fight our way into oblivion rather than consider the (unimaginable) alternative of

TRY TO IMAGINE WHO YOU REALLY ARE.

giving up violence as a way of life. Meanwhile, the soul, the heart of the nation, gets blue. We can spare little money for welfare, the old, the sick, the exceptional. Stagflation is that peculiar form of corporate neurosis in which depression and inflation are simultaneous. The reds are filled with grandiose ideas of a Pax Americana, astronomical spending, stimulating the economy. The blues see our cities, families, our bonds of intimacy deteriorating.

One old soldier, Dwight D. Eisenhower, saw the problem clearly and warned against the military-industrial complex when he left office: "Every gun that is made, every warship launched, every rocket fired, signifies, in the final sense, a theft from those who hunger and are not fed, those who are cold and are not clothed. This world in arms is not spending money alone. It is spending the sweat of its laborers, the genius of its scientists, the hopes of its children."

Life organized around "the enemy" provides superficial excitement and profound despair. The only thing paranoids can imagine is who is threatening them, never who would like to stroke, caress, comfort, or enjoy them. The man who has to have an enemy is psychologically impoverished. He is too poor in imagination or compassion to feel the bond of friendship.

The most sterile places in the world are the war rooms. Generals, specialists in violence, defenders of the faith against the enemy, focus all their energies on deadly scenarios. The warrior mentality has brought us to the point of tragic absurdity. Glasnost and the collapse of communism notwithstanding, we are prepared for a nuclear "interchange" in which half the world's population might be destroyed.

When the blessed crisis comes, adrenaline flows in tough-minded men as they imagine the bloodbath. Daniel Ellsberg described the scene to me: "The excitement of being in the war

IN WAR WE ARE PRISONERS OF DEATH.

room in a crisis is tremendous. You are wired into everything that's happening. You can see those people who have been denied access wandering around like zombies who have been unplugged from the excitement. They are still dreaming of some way to get back into the wild excitement, that delicious knuckle-cracking tension of contemplating Doomsday. This kind of thing literally becomes addictive. Beside it ordinary life is pale and lacks excitement."

War may be hell, but it is also, from a certain perspective, the essence of tedium. Killing is an unimaginative, predictable, and banal way of dealing with problems. Violence is repetition compulsion. Nobody ever learns, wins, or solves anything by warfare. Nations drain their resources generation after generation. If history teaches us anything, it is that war (the refuge of the impotent, the unimaginative, and the unfeeling) is conducted by the already dead—psychological zombies whose entire repertoire of passion has been reduced to violence.

In human intercourse, excitement begins with forgiveness. Only forgiveness sets us free from the locked-in compulsive cycle of suspicion-hurt-retaliation and allows us to turn our gaze away from the single enemy to the kaleidoscopic possibilities that surround us. Enmity hardens the heart, narrows the focus of the eyes, constricts muscles and blood vessels. Assume the posture of fight-or-flight and blood pressure goes up and everything in the nervous system is focused on a single point of danger. Trust softens the body, dilates the arteries, widens the eyes, allows us to open up and welcome the surroundings.

Can we break the violence habit? Create a politics of hope to replace the politics of violence-boredom?

Imagine what could happen if we had a politics dominated by imagination and compassion rather than paranoia and violence.

PARANOIDS LOVE THEIR ENEMIES.

De-escalation is a risk—but an interesting risk. The habit of violence yields certain results—depression, destruction, death. The arms race presents us with a momentous choice: either we exhaust our life force or we wake up from the nightmare of violence. Our current epidemic of psychological and economic depression cannot be cured by stimulating the economy, tranquilizing the mind, elevating the mood of the body politic with rhetoric. Our blues are real. Our major expenditures of energy and imagination are invested in the business of killing. "For over a generation, approximately half of all our scientists and engineers in the country have worked on military-related projects. As a result, the United States has the most advanced missiles and warplanes, but we cannot build a decent railroad."[6] That's depressing.

The only just war is the battle against our tendency to do battle. The righteous war is against the powers within the self and the nation that keep us in continual conflict. The true enemy is within. So is the Kingdom of Peace. What is fearful is our own fear of freedom and fullness of life.

There are moments in human history that are pivotal. We are at the fork. The future of our emotional and psychological lives depends upon our political decisions. Either oblivion or the risk of peace.

BEYOND THE POLITICS OF DEPRESSION

The problems we have touched are so vast in scope we are all but paralyzed when we search for solutions. How would we go about valuing and granting full equality to the woman's way of being? Re-creating work and discovering vocation? Cooling our

IMAGINATION AND COMPASSION ARE THE FIRST CASUALTIES OF WAR.

lust for violence? Ending the insanity of war? Reforming the media? Creating a society in which plurality of imagination, desire, and life-style are genuinely encouraged? To suggest that we make massive changes in the way we construct our relationships, communities, work, and warfare may seem naive and utopian at best. But what is the alternative? More depression. More consumption. More violence.

In politics, as in psychotherapy, the cure begins with accepting the dis-ease as a signal of a deep crisis in value and imagination. Our nameless sadness is telling us that it's time to mourn the passing of the old American dream, to admit candidly that our civil religion with its vision of "liberty and justice for all" has been replaced by the commercial creed of products and profit for all. Our bottom line has become the gross national product. Vietnam was the end of our innocence. The energy crisis, the emergence of new forms of nationalism, and the proliferation of nuclear weapons point to the end of American pretensions to omnipotence.

We may be at the end or the beginning of the American Revolution. We may become increasingly militaristic and fascistic as we try to grasp the lion's share of the world's declining resources. Or we may experience a new awakening, discover a new dream. We might kick the speed trip and learn to enjoy less wasteful rhythms. We might learn to mark value by our capacity to enjoy the profound simplicities—clean air, pure water, satisfying work, touching, sharing food, walking, watching children grow, conversation, silence, planting, tending, harvesting, craftsmanship, making useful things and beautiful machines, creating

IN A DEMOCRACY, WAR SHOULD BE LEFT TO GENERALISTS.

careful communities. We may find in voluntary simplicity more pleasure than we once took in conspicuous consumption.

The New American Revolution, if there is to be one, will be the work of many generations. For machine lovers to learn to cohabit in peace with all species of life is a new adventure. Perhaps our blues are only the first notes of a distant song that is beginning to sound through us. If we listen carefully, we may hear a new future calling us through our dis-ease.

WAR IS A BLOODY BORE.

NOTES

Chapter 1
The Boredom Epidemic

1. *Harper's*, No. 62, November 1962.
2. Quoted in Elwin Powell, *The Design of Discord*, Oxford University Press, 1970, p. 172.
3. Bertrand Russell, *The Conquest of Happiness*, New York: Book League of America, 1930, p. 60.

Chapter 2
A Short History of the Blues and the Noontide Demon

1. Bertrand Russell, *The Conquest of Happiness*, New York: Book League of America, 1930.
2. Reinhard Kuhn, *The Demon of Noontide*, Princeton, NJ: Princeton University Press, 1976.

Chapter 5
Fatigue: The Personal Energy Crisis

1. *The New England Journal of Medicine*, April 1944.
2. *The Journal of Psychosomatic Research*, No. 11, 1967. © Pergamon Press.

Chapter 6
Simple Boredom: Monotony

1. *Scientific American*, 196: 52–56.

Chapter 7
Chronic Boredom

1. *The Collected Papers of Otto Fenichel*, New York: W. W. Norton, 1953.
2. Quoted in Kuhn, *The Demon of Noontide*, p. 326.
3. "Fear of Action As an Essential Element in the Sentiment of Melancholia," in *Feeling and Emotion*, Worcester, Mass.: Clark University Press, 1928.
4. Stephen Vincent Benét, *John Brown's Body*, New York: Rinehart & Co., 1927.
5. *Bulletin of the Atomic Scientists*, November 1975.

Chapter 8
The Deepening Darkness:
Depression and Apathy

1. *The New York Times Magazine*, February 12, 1972.

Chapter 9
The Joyful Art of Doing Nothing

1. *Science Digest*, December 1972.
2. Chögyam Trungpa, *The Myth of Freedom*, Berkeley, Calif.: Shambala Press, 1976, p. 55f.
3. Quoted in Gabriel Marcel, *Homo Viator*, New York: Harper & Row, 1962, p. 28.
4. Russell, *The Conquest of Happiness*, p. 61f.
5. Nancy Ross, ed., *The World of Zen*, New York: Random House, 1960, p. 84.

Chapter 11
The Renewal of Imagination and Desire

1. Quoted in Sam Keen, *Voices and Visions*, New York: Harper & Row, 1976, p. 97.

Chapter 12
Feeling Alive: Unfreezing E-motions

1. Norman O. Brown, *Love's Body*, New York: Random House, 1966.

Chapter 13
Risk Taking

1. *Psychology Today*, October 1974.

Chapter 14
From Sex to Intimacy

1. Milton Mayeroff, *On Caring*, New York: Harper & Row, 1971.

Chapter 15
The Politics of Depression and Hope

1. Maggie Scarf, "The More Sorrowful Sex," *Psychology Today*, April 1979.
2. *Psychology Today*, May 1978.
3. Wendell Berry, *The Unsettling of America*, New York: Avon Books, 1978.
4. Peter Chowka, *New Age*, April 1979.
5. Gene Youngblood, "The Mass Media and the Future of Desire," *CoEvolution Quarterly*, Winter 1977.
6. "SANE Reports," *The Washington Spectator*, February 1, 1979.

INDEX